THE ART OF
Palmistry

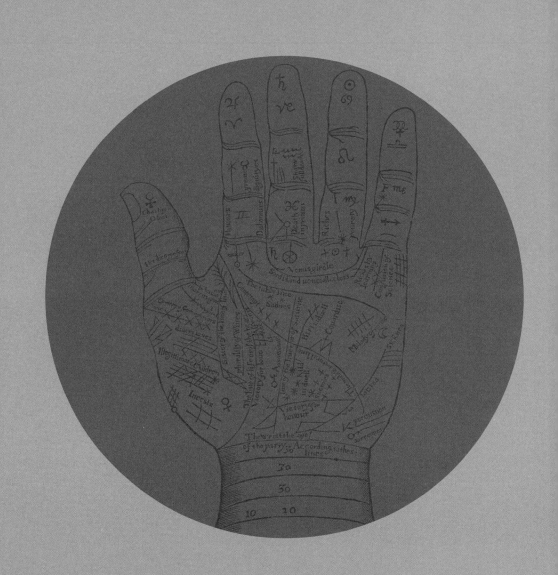

THE ART OF

Palmistry

A practical guide to reading your fortune

Edited by
ANNA SOUTHGATE

STERLING ETHOS
New York

STERLING ETHOS
New York

An Imprint of Sterling Publishing Co., Inc.
1166 Avenue of the Americas
New York, NY 10036

ISBN 978-1-4549-2149-3

For information about custom editions, special sales, and
premium and corporate purchases, please contact Sterling
Special Sales at 800-805-5489 or specialsales@
sterlingpublishing.com.

Manufactured in China

2 4 6 8 10 9 7 5 3 1

www.sterlingpublishing.com

CONTENTS

INTRODUCTION

Every person has a unique life story, and our hands contain the coded information that tells us what makes each of us different. A new palm is the palmist's equivalent of a new book, with its own fascinating story to tell.

Palmistry, also known as chiromancy and hand analysis, is the most personal of the self-discovery systems. It helps us to understand our personalities, potential, talents, strengths, abilities, and limitations. Also, the lines on your hands will change over time, revealing new information, so you will be able to consult this book time and time again.

By comparing features of your palm with the photographs of hands in this book, you will be able to build up a palm profile and monitor its changing patterns. This is a working book. You can use the book when you have decisions to make, and referring to it regularly will help you to map the changes in your life.

A huge amount of information is displayed in your hands, and palmistry is the key that unlocks and translates the secrets of who you really are, revealing your past, present, and potential for the future. Palmistry is all about you and what is most important to you—whether it be money, love, your career, and so on. You can be your own personal therapist. With every palm reading session, you will begin to feel that you understand yourself a little better. You will learn to minimize your weaknesses and take advantage of your strengths.

Making decisions

- ◆ Palmistry helps you to find your professional path.

- ◆ It answers questions by unlocking secrets and reviving memories.

- ◆ Palmistry helps you move toward personal growth.

- ◆ It encourages self-understanding, and generates new thoughts and ideas.

- ◆ It helps you to recognize mindtraps and to overcome unproductive thinking.

- ◆ Palmistry reveals opportunities.

- ◆ It helps to sharpen and clear the mind.

▶ Woodcut illustration showing the main lines and mounts of the palm from **Antropologium de Hominis Dignitate**, published in 1501 by German physician Magnus Hundt.

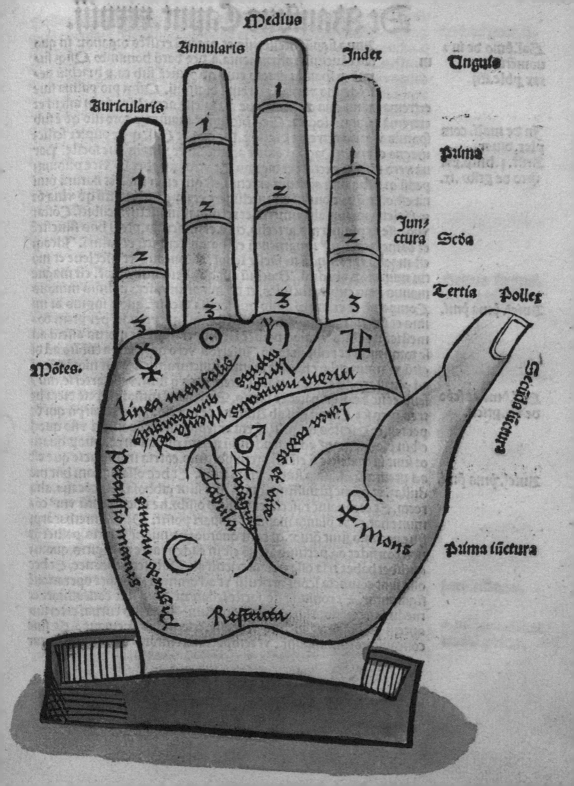

TYPES OF PALMISTRY

The hands are home to a disproportionately high number of the body's nerve-ending receptors. This makes your palms the best place to chart physical, emotional, and medical history, intellect, potential achievement, and changes in your life's path. The basic principles of the art of palm reading are described over the next few pages.

There are three basic types of palmistry: Oriental palmistry, Asian palmistry, and Western palmistry. Oriental and Asian palmistry rely heavily on skin patterns, fingertip patterns, symbols with the appearance of animals, and the lines that run around the wrist called the rascettes or bracelets of life. These types of palmistry focus on the extended family and on everyday decisions much more than Western palmistry. The main focus of Western palmistry is you.

Which hand do you read?

You should do a reading for both hands—one correlates to your inner personality and the other to your outward personality. By comparing the readings of each hand you will have an idea of how your actual life matches or differs from your inner potential.

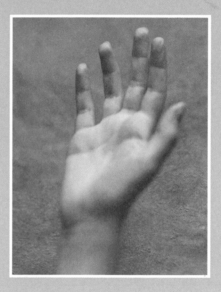

THE PASSIVE HAND
This is your non-writing hand and reveals the unconscious self—your inner personality, your life's potential, and your family medical history.

THE DOMINANT HAND
This is the hand you write with and reveals the conscious self—your outward personality, what you have made and will make of your life, and your medical history.

◀ **A Fortune-teller Reading the Palm of a Soldier,** by Pietro della Vecchia, 1602.

CHANGING YOUR PATH
Remember, the future is not cast in stone. Humans are powerful creatures that can and do change the paths they follow. Lines can break, breaks can heal, and lines can become weaker or stronger. Some lines will change within a few weeks; others will change fundamentally over a few years.

SETTING THE SCENE

For the best and most enjoyable palm readings, you must be completely at ease. Try to choose a time of day when you are less likely to be disturbed. Create a relaxed and stress-free atmosphere with natural light or soft lighting at night. Shine a desk light across the palm to enhance detail. Soft, pleasant music and lightly scented candles will help create the right mood. A magnifying glass is useful to see details both in the hand you are reading and the palms in this book. A soft pillow to rest your hand on with the palm facing upward will help the hand to adopt its natural position.

Mindset

Before you start your reading, relax, breathe deeply, and clear your mind. You do not need to be psychic. It is a matter of simply interpreting the lines and translating them as you would from one language to another. If you keep an open mind, you will achieve much, much more. Your hands are the book of your life.

Starting a reading

You will need a sheet of acetate and a water-based fiber-tip pen.

1 Place your dominant hand palm down onto the sheet of acetate and draw around it. Turn your hand and the acetate over and mark the main lines. (You can reposition and mark more of your lines later.)

2 Using the Instant Identifier on pages 18–29, match the shape of each line to one of the many examples. To find out the meanings, refer to the indicated pages that show the closest match for each line on your hand. Result: your very own palm reading!

3 Photocopy the acetate and write down the date, then wipe the acetate clean and start again with the passive hand. Where the lines differ, interpret the lines on the passive hand as features of the inner person or latent self.

4 If you experience any difficulty drawing and interpreting several lines together, simply start again with the outline of the hand and just work on one line at a time.

5 For an in-depth reading, follow the same procedure but take care to draw breaks, islands, and other markings as accurately as possible. Details of the specific markings are all found in this book. Check each line carefully and you will build up a full and accurate palm reading.

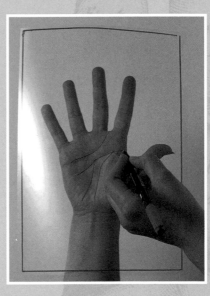

▲ Place a sheet of acetate over your hand and draw the main lines onto it. If you find it difficult, ask a friend to help you.

Remember to repeat the process with your passive hand for a more complete reading.

MAPPING THE HAND

THE MAIN LINES

The lines on your hand are indicators of major influences and movements in your life. Identify each line on your palm by checking its position and path. Remember that not every line will show up on different palms.

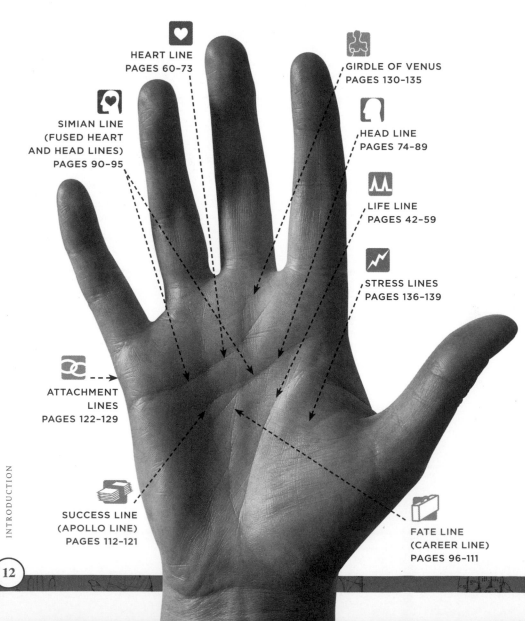

HEART LINE
PAGES 60–73

SIMIAN LINE
(FUSED HEART
AND HEAD LINES)
PAGES 90–95

GIRDLE OF VENUS
PAGES 130–135

HEAD LINE
PAGES 74–89

LIFE LINE
PAGES 42–59

STRESS LINES
PAGES 136–139

ATTACHMENT
LINES
PAGES 122–129

SUCCESS LINE
(APOLLO LINE)
PAGES 112–121

FATE LINE
(CAREER LINE)
PAGES 96–111

Assessing lines

The quality of each line and the patterns that are formed around it are the signs that will help you to do your interpretation and make your reading. One useful working theory for assessing lines is to imagine each line as a steadily flowing river. A clearly defined, even line is a river and a life running smoothly. This may help you to remember the subtle changes in meaning that each line variation brings. Are you in for a bumpy ride? Is the river blocked and do you need to go another way?

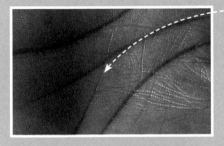

UNEVEN LINE
Uneven lines are deep in some places, showing strength and intensity, and shallow in others, showing spent energy and weakness.

SPLIT LINE
A line that splits, with branches running close to the main line then stopping, shows energy wasted on unfinished projects. A wide, long branch leading to a mount shows attraction to the qualities of that mount.

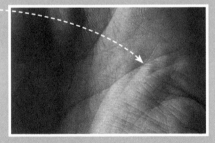

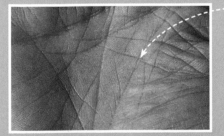

ISLANDS
An island is formed by a line splitting from a main line then rejoining it. Islands show energy weakened by flowing in two directions, then strength of purpose renewed as the lines combine.

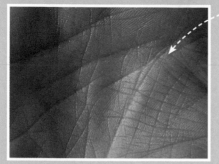

BREAKS

Breaks stop the natural flow in some way. A small break or overlapping broken ends will have a minimal effect.

SQUARES

A square is a protective barrier that forms particularly around a break or weakness in a line, like a reinforcement on a riverbank. This indicates that someone is caring for you in times of difficulty.

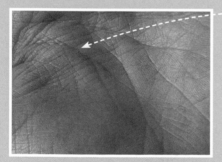

CHAINED LINE

A chained line shows a path that is labored, strained, or obstructed in some way. Think of that river with its force divided. Chaining on the heart line shows sentimentality, and on the head line shows that you are prone to headaches.

SISTER LINES

A line appearing alongside and parallel to weakness on another line is called a sister line, and protects and strengthens the main line.

PALM SIGNS

Signs or symbols may be found on the palm in several places. The interpretations of the symbols that follow have been proven right time and time again.

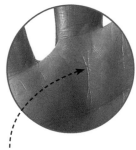

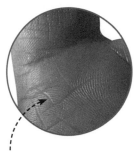

TRIANGLES
An isolated triangle on the palm shows great mental brilliance. A triangle on the mount at the base of the index finger highlights lofty ambition.

STARS
Stars illuminate. When a star appears in any area—formed by three lines crossing at a single point—it signifies brighter, better, and generally more fortunate prospects.

SQUARES
A notable square, found on the mount at the base of the index finger, is the teacher's square. This indicates a person whose talent lies in teaching and coaching.

PHALANXES OF THE THUMB

The top phalanx of the thumb, which contains the nail, represents willpower. The lower phalanx, below the joint, represents logic. Normally, they are about the same length. A shorter top phalanx shows a lack of willpower. A long lower phalanx denotes a very logical person. Lines cutting across the lower phalanx are called intuition rings—the more rings there are, the greater the intuition. These lines often signify the seemingly contradictory condition of a very logical, yet highly intuitive individual.

Fingerprint patterns

Every person's fingerprint patterns, as we know from their use in police department records, are unique. They can give us further clues to a person's nature and strengths.

ULNAR LOOP

The ulnar loop points toward the thumb and is the most common fingerprint pattern. It shows someone who is adaptable and versatile in changing circumstances.

RADIAL LOOP

The radial loop points away from the thumb and shows a versatile, adaptable, and also rather extroverted personality.

COMPOSITE LOOP

The composite loop looks like the letter S, with two loops lying in opposite directions. This shows an often indecisive individual who sees both sides of a problem and is pulled in both directions.

WHORL (ISLAND)

A whorl looks like the ripples made by a stone dropped into a pond, and indicates people who "island" themselves by concentrating solely on a particular task. This usually means a leader or a nonconformist who holds strong personal views, and often denotes success, particularly when seen on the index and/or ring finger.

ARCH

A small arch denotes the need to provide protection and security, and shows a person who is driven to a sense of responsibility, but often feels it as a burden. The arch, though infrequent, usually appears on more than one finger, exaggerating its effect.

PEACOCK'S EYE

This is a whorl enclosed in a loop. The characteristics are the same as for the whorl but the loop adds luck, protection, and penetrating perception.

CHILDREN LINES

These are the lines that cross the attachment lines at right angles. Recent palmistry research has shown no conclusive correlation between children lines and the number of children you are likely to have. Perhaps today, the children lines reflect potential rather than actual children in a world where contraception, greater emphasis on career, and increased negative stress affect people's decision or capacity to have children. As a result, children lines signify your level of empathy with children.

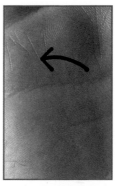

PALMAR RIDGES

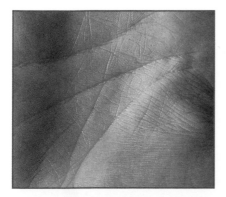

Fingerprint patterns as they appear on the palm are known as palmar ridges. As a general rule, your body is in good balance when the skin ridges on your palm are clear and the skin is springy when pressed with a finger. Examination of the palmar ridges can reveal a variety of imbalances and health conditions.

MAPPING THE HAND

This section shows a reduced reproduction of all the palms featured in this book and is designed to help you find a quick match for your palm. Trace your palm on the acetate sheet (see page 11), look through the reduced palms and read to find the closest match, then turn to the page number listed. Below are some frequently asked questions to help you get the most from your readings.

Q: MY LIFE LINE HAS A HIGH START AND A FORKED END. IN WHICH SECTION DO I LOOK?

A: Look in both sections. Any line can comprise more than one set of features. Simply combine the interpretations for each feature to make a fuller reading. The examples in this book are designed to show each feature at its clearest, but there are many variations.

Q: WHY ARE THERE SO MANY LINES ON MY HAND?

A: Probably because you have a full hand. First, compare your hand to the hands in the stress lines section. Finding the dominant lines through a maze of stress lines is a common problem for palmists today. The best way to tackle this is to carefully examine each line one at a time.

Q: WHAT HAPPENS TO THE LINES WHEN I MAKE A MAJOR LIFE CHANGE?

A: Lines on your hand change over time. If you make a major life change that is not shown on your palm map, the lines will change accordingly within a few months. It is worth making a photocopy of your hand with some current notes, then monitor changes as they happen.

Q: MY LINES ARE NOT EXACTLY THE SAME AS ON THE CLOSEST MATCHING PALM. WHAT DOES THIS MEAN?

A: Lines vary from person to person. The palms in this book have been chosen to illustrate the most important features. The additional information for each hand may or may not apply to you, so browse through other pages to spot features that match your own.

Q: I HAVE JUST A FEW LINES. DOES THIS MEAN MY LIFE IS FAIRLY UNINTERESTING?

A: There is no such thing as a boring palm. Each palm has a unique, fascinating story, which the palmist is privileged to glimpse. Having just a few lines often makes readings more straightforward.

THE MOUNTS

PAGES 30–41

JUPITER MOUNT
◆ Well-developed

PAGE 32

SATURN MOUNT
◆ Well-developed

PAGE 33

APOLLO MOUNT
◆ Well-developed

PAGE 34

MERCURY MOUNT
◆ Well-developed

PAGE 35

VENUS MOUNT
◆ Well-developed

PAGE 36

LUNA MOUNT
◆ Well-developed

PAGE 37

NEPTUNE MOUNT
◆ Well-developed

PAGE 38

MARS NEGATIVE MOUNT
◆ Well-developed

PAGE 39

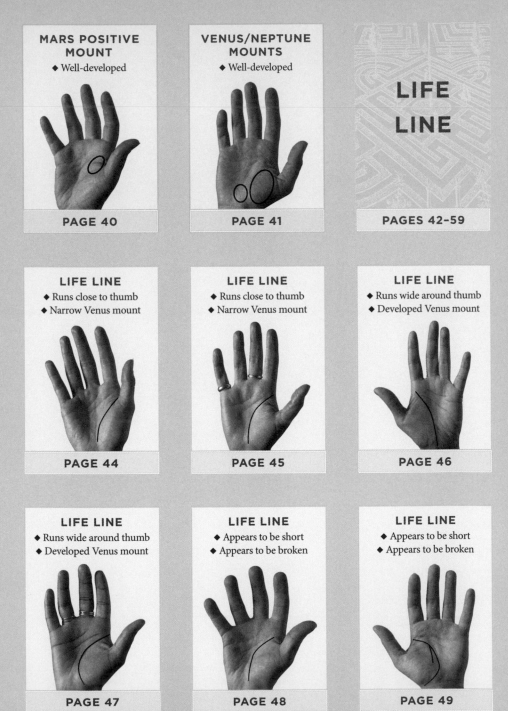

MARS POSITIVE MOUNT
◆ Well-developed

PAGE 40

VENUS/NEPTUNE MOUNTS
◆ Well-developed

PAGE 41

LIFE LINE

PAGES 42–59

LIFE LINE
◆ Runs close to thumb
◆ Narrow Venus mount

PAGE 44

LIFE LINE
◆ Runs close to thumb
◆ Narrow Venus mount

PAGE 45

LIFE LINE
◆ Runs wide around thumb
◆ Developed Venus mount

PAGE 46

LIFE LINE
◆ Runs wide around thumb
◆ Developed Venus mount

PAGE 47

LIFE LINE
◆ Appears to be short
◆ Appears to be broken

PAGE 48

LIFE LINE
◆ Appears to be short
◆ Appears to be broken

PAGE 49

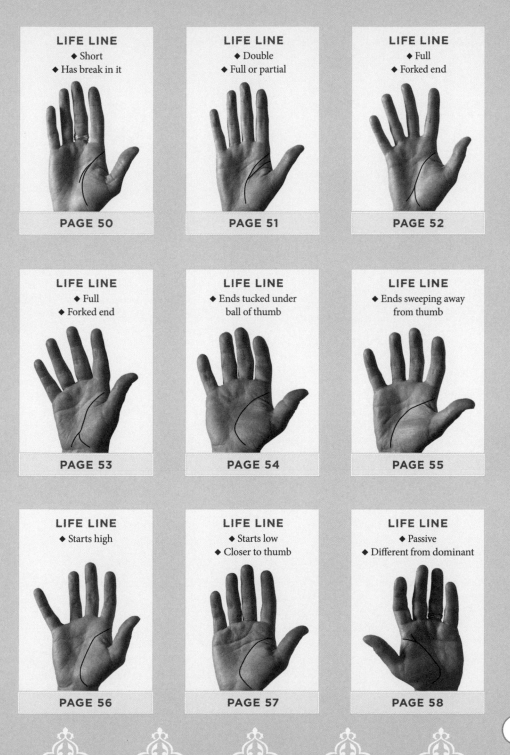

LIFE LINE
◆ Short
◆ Has break in it

PAGE 50

LIFE LINE
◆ Double
◆ Full or partial

PAGE 51

LIFE LINE
◆ Full
◆ Forked end

PAGE 52

LIFE LINE
◆ Full
◆ Forked end

PAGE 53

LIFE LINE
◆ Ends tucked under
 ball of thumb

PAGE 54

LIFE LINE
◆ Ends sweeping away
 from thumb

PAGE 55

LIFE LINE
◆ Starts high

PAGE 56

LIFE LINE
◆ Starts low
◆ Closer to thumb

PAGE 57

LIFE LINE
◆ Passive
◆ Different from dominant

PAGE 58

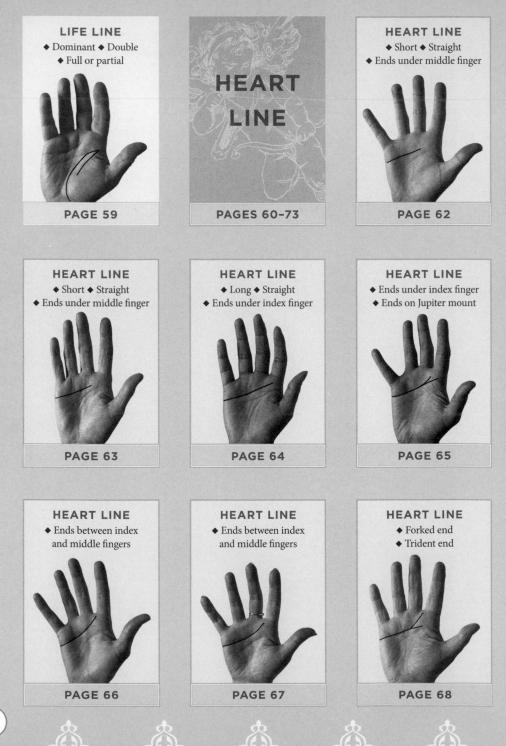

LIFE LINE
- ◆ Dominant ◆ Double
- ◆ Full or partial

PAGE 59

HEART
LINE

PAGES 60–73

HEART LINE
- ◆ Short ◆ Straight
- ◆ Ends under middle finger

PAGE 62

HEART LINE
- ◆ Short ◆ Straight
- ◆ Ends under middle finger

PAGE 63

HEART LINE
- ◆ Long ◆ Straight
- ◆ Ends under index finger

PAGE 64

HEART LINE
- ◆ Ends under index finger
- ◆ Ends on Jupiter mount

PAGE 65

HEART LINE
- ◆ Ends between index and middle fingers

PAGE 66

HEART LINE
- ◆ Ends between index and middle fingers

PAGE 67

HEART LINE
- ◆ Forked end
- ◆ Trident end

PAGE 68

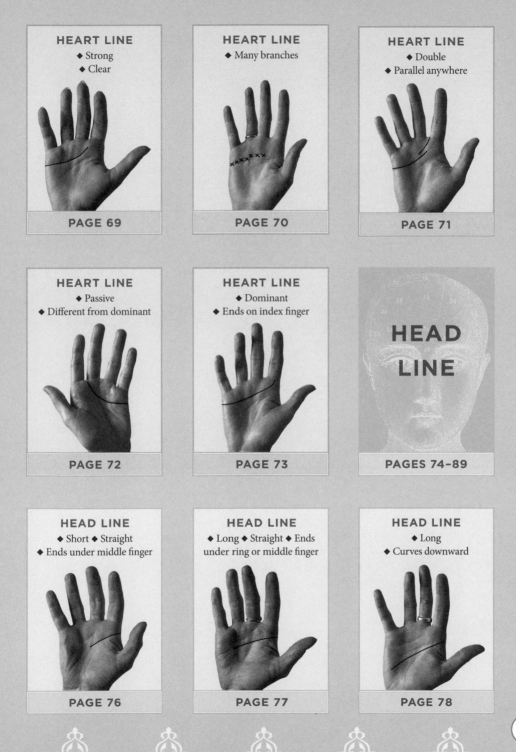

HEART LINE
- ◆ Strong
- ◆ Clear

PAGE 69

HEART LINE
- ◆ Many branches

PAGE 70

HEART LINE
- ◆ Double
- ◆ Parallel anywhere

PAGE 71

HEART LINE
- ◆ Passive
- ◆ Different from dominant

PAGE 72

HEART LINE
- ◆ Dominant
- ◆ Ends on index finger

PAGE 73

HEAD LINE

PAGES 74–89

HEAD LINE
- ◆ Short ◆ Straight
- ◆ Ends under middle finger

PAGE 76

HEAD LINE
- ◆ Long ◆ Straight ◆ Ends under ring or middle finger

PAGE 77

HEAD LINE
- ◆ Long
- ◆ Curves downward

PAGE 78

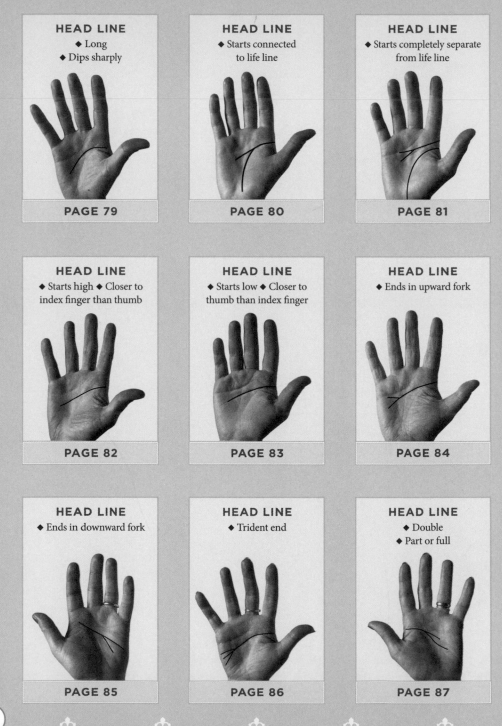

HEAD LINE
- ◆ Long
- ◆ Dips sharply

PAGE 79

HEAD LINE
- ◆ Starts connected to life line

PAGE 80

HEAD LINE
- ◆ Starts completely separate from life line

PAGE 81

HEAD LINE
- ◆ Starts high ◆ Closer to index finger than thumb

PAGE 82

HEAD LINE
- ◆ Starts low ◆ Closer to thumb than index finger

PAGE 83

HEAD LINE
- ◆ Ends in upward fork

PAGE 84

HEAD LINE
- ◆ Ends in downward fork

PAGE 85

HEAD LINE
- ◆ Trident end

PAGE 86

HEAD LINE
- ◆ Double
- ◆ Part or full

PAGE 87

INSTANT IDENTIFIER

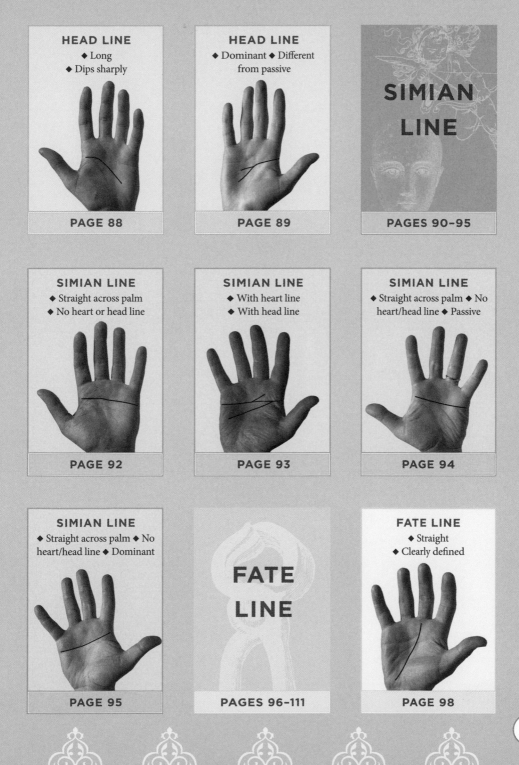

HEAD LINE
- ◆ Long
- ◆ Dips sharply

PAGE 88

HEAD LINE
- ◆ Dominant ◆ Different from passive

PAGE 89

SIMIAN LINE

PAGES 90–95

SIMIAN LINE
- ◆ Straight across palm
- ◆ No heart or head line

PAGE 92

SIMIAN LINE
- ◆ With heart line
- ◆ With head line

PAGE 93

SIMIAN LINE
- ◆ Straight across palm ◆ No heart/head line ◆ Passive

PAGE 94

SIMIAN LINE
- ◆ Straight across palm ◆ No heart/head line ◆ Dominant

PAGE 95

FATE LINE

PAGES 96–111

FATE LINE
- ◆ Straight
- ◆ Clearly defined

PAGE 98

FATE LINE
◆ Appears to stop and start

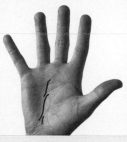

PAGE 99

FATE LINE
◆ Starts high on palm

PAGE 100

FATE LINE
◆ Starts on Luna mount

PAGE 101

FATE LINE
◆ Stops far short of base of fingers

PAGE 102

FATE LINE
◆ Ends high on palm
◆ Stops at base of fingers

PAGE 103

FATE LINE
◆ Ends toward index finger

PAGE 104

FATE LINE
◆ With a line striking it
◆ Upward joining branch

PAGE 105

FATE LINE
◆ Starts on Venus mount

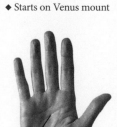

PAGE 106

FATE LINE
◆ Multiple ends

PAGE 107

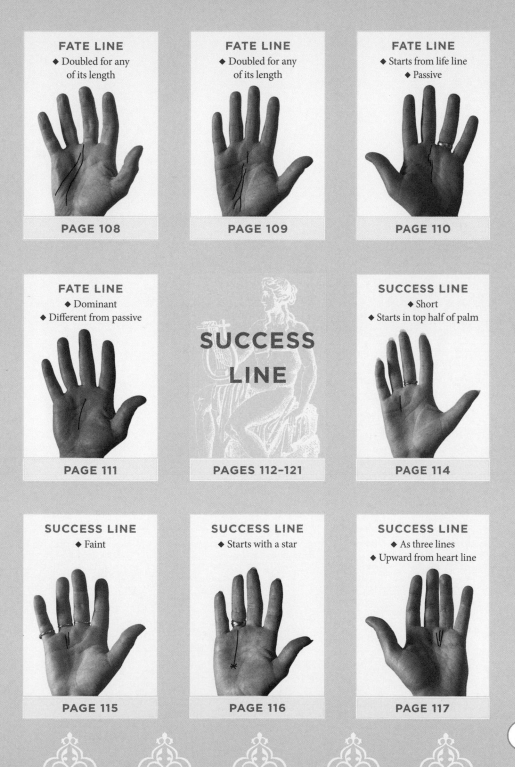

FATE LINE
◆ Doubled for any
of its length

PAGE 108

FATE LINE
◆ Doubled for any
of its length

PAGE 109

FATE LINE
◆ Starts from life line
◆ Passive

PAGE 110

FATE LINE
◆ Dominant
◆ Different from passive

PAGE 111

SUCCESS LINE

PAGES 112–121

SUCCESS LINE
◆ Short
◆ Starts in top half of palm

PAGE 114

SUCCESS LINE
◆ Faint

PAGE 115

SUCCESS LINE
◆ Starts with a star

PAGE 116

SUCCESS LINE
◆ As three lines
◆ Upward from heart line

PAGE 117

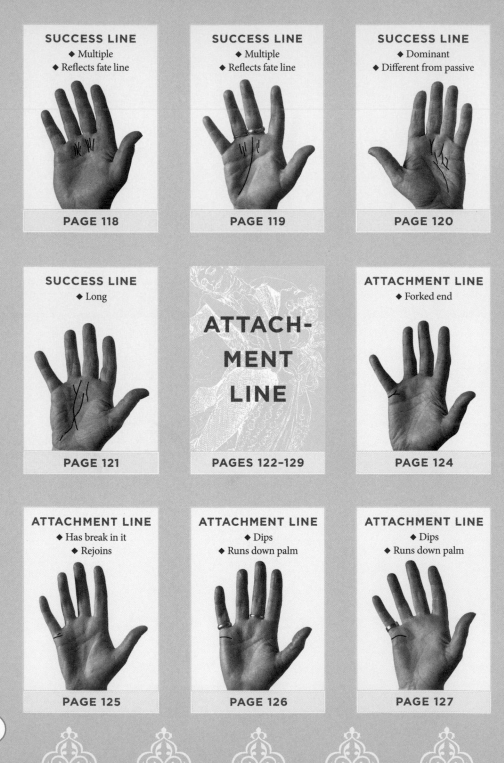

SUCCESS LINE
- ◆ Multiple
- ◆ Reflects fate line

PAGE 118

SUCCESS LINE
- ◆ Multiple
- ◆ Reflects fate line

PAGE 119

SUCCESS LINE
- ◆ Dominant
- ◆ Different from passive

PAGE 120

SUCCESS LINE
- ◆ Long

PAGE 121

ATTACH-MENT LINE

PAGES 122–129

ATTACHMENT LINE
- ◆ Forked end

PAGE 124

ATTACHMENT LINE
- ◆ Has break in it
- ◆ Rejoins

PAGE 125

ATTACHMENT LINE
- ◆ Dips
- ◆ Runs down palm

PAGE 126

ATTACHMENT LINE
- ◆ Dips
- ◆ Runs down palm

PAGE 127

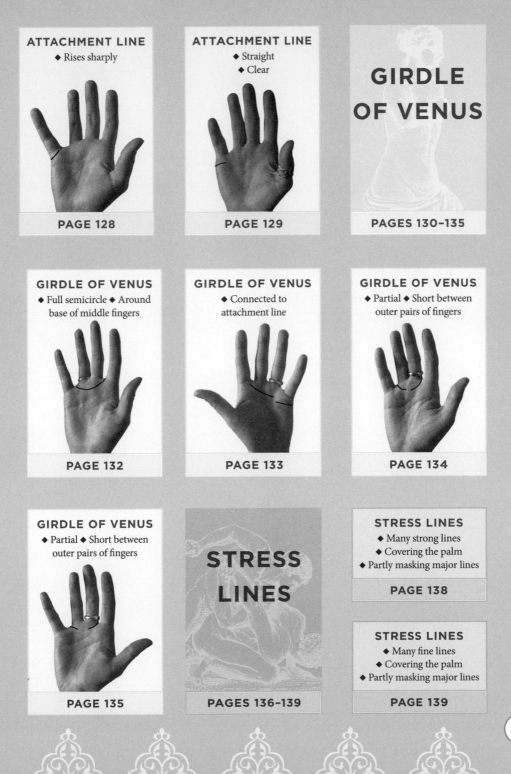

ATTACHMENT LINE
- ◆ Rises sharply

PAGE 128

ATTACHMENT LINE
- ◆ Straight
- ◆ Clear

PAGE 129

GIRDLE OF VENUS

PAGES 130–135

GIRDLE OF VENUS
- ◆ Full semicircle ◆ Around base of middle fingers

PAGE 132

GIRDLE OF VENUS
- ◆ Connected to attachment line

PAGE 133

GIRDLE OF VENUS
- ◆ Partial ◆ Short between outer pairs of fingers

PAGE 134

GIRDLE OF VENUS
- ◆ Partial ◆ Short between outer pairs of fingers

PAGE 135

STRESS LINES

PAGES 136–139

STRESS LINES
- ◆ Many strong lines
- ◆ Covering the palm
- ◆ Partly masking major lines

PAGE 138

STRESS LINES
- ◆ Many fine lines
- ◆ Covering the palm
- ◆ Partly masking major lines

PAGE 139

THE MOUNTS

What drives you?

LOCATION

MAJOR MOUNTS

◆ **Jupiter:** At base of index finger.

◆ **Saturn:** At base of middle finger.

◆ **Apollo:** At base of ring finger.

◆ **Mercury:** At base of little finger.

◆ **Venus:** At base of thumb.

◆ **Luna:** At opposite edge of palm from Venus mount.

MINOR MOUNTS

◆ **Neptune:** Between Venus and Luna mounts, and adjacent to wrist.

◆ **Mars negative:** At side of palm opposite to thumb, between Luna and Mercury mounts.

◆ **Mars positive:** At side of palm between index finger and thumb.

MEANING

Mounts represent the driving forces in your life. The most developed mounts on your palm, the dominant mounts, are the ones that most affect you. Feeling your mounts to determine their size is called mount manipulation and is a wonderful and soothing activity, whether you have it done for you or you do it for others. Initially, the best way to find your dominant mounts is to use a light, exploratory touch to locate the padded areas of your palm without actually looking at it. When you have a rough idea of the areas that feel more swollen or raised, gently cup your palm and look at it. You will be able to see the mounts stand out. Do not worry if the mounts at the base of the fingers seem offset; this is completely normal.

Five Common Questions

◆ Why do I feel the need to work hard and play hard?

◆ Am I a natural-born leader?

◆ Why is communication most important to me?

◆ I often sit daydreaming and constructing novels in my mind. What does it mean?

◆ Why do I need people around me to "come alive"?

Jupiter mount
Saturn mount
Apollo mount
Mars positive
Mercury mount
Venus mount
Mars negative
Neptune mount
Luna mount

◆ WELL-DEVELOPED

You are wise and have great business acumen and leadership qualities. A full mount of Jupiter is often associated with island fingerprint patterns. The development of the mount slightly toward the middle finger shows high morals and a well-developed sense of justice and ambition. An overdeveloped mount indicates that these personal characteristics have become exaggerated—generosity has become extravagance, and enterprise has become pompous self-importance or arrogance.

MYSTIC CROSS
In the quadrangle formed between the heart and head lines, your mystic cross highlights an interest in the occult or paranormal or the rediscovery of a psychic gift. You have great intuition or a sixth sense, manifested in business deals, often of a speculative nature.

COMPLEMENTARY READINGS

RAJA LOOP
The loop pattern between your index and middle fingers was historically thought to denote a blood connection with royalty. This is a unique sign.

LUNA MOUNT
A developed lower Luna mount, appearing almost to overhang your wrist, is another sign of someone particularly gifted and perceptive.

JUPITER MOUNT

SATURN MOUNT 〜

◆ WELL-DEVELOPED

Stability, seriousness, and a love of tradition in your life are emphasized. A high mount can mean an overserious predisposition and stern outlook, but the gently rounded mount here is more likely to show your interest in study and research, or perhaps reveals an unnecessarily pessimistic view of marriage prospects. Despite the stern implications of a developed Saturn mount, the opposite picture—a warm personality—appears in your hand.

COMPLEMENTARY READINGS

RINGS
Wearing rings on your middle finger is a cry from the heart for security, perhaps within a marriage.

ARCH
The arch fingerprint pattern on your index finger shows a strong desire to protect everyone and everything around you.

APOLLO MOUNT
Your Apollo mount is also developed, which shows your sunny outlook and attractive personality.

LIFE LINE
Your life line runs wide, showing that you are a "people" person, with a wide circle of friends.

VENUS MOUNT
Your rounded Venus mount shows warmth and vitality.

SATURN MOUNT

◆ WELL-DEVELOPED

Associated with money, fun, enjoyment, recreation, and success, your developed Apollo mount shows you to have a definite talent for television work. You are unfailingly optimistic, and there is a strong chance that fortune will shine on you and everything you do.

APOLLO MOUNT

COMPLEMENTARY READINGS

FATE LINE
Although there are a number of twists and turns throughout your career, it is significant that both a success line and a business line spring from your fate line. A little work effort will go a long way toward success.

LIFE LINE
In your mid to late teens, there is a break in your life line with a connection to a stronger line running wide around the ball of your thumb. An emigration to a new life with more comfort and a wider range of prospects is a strong possibility.

VIA LASCIVIA
The horizontal, low line running from the edge of the palm away from the thumb is known as a via lascivia. Historically misunderstood as a sign of a debauched lifestyle, today this is known as an allergies line, indicating a sensitivity to stimulants.

MERCURY MOUNT

◆ WELL-DEVELOPED

You are a great communicator with a keen working intuition. A developed Mercury mount also reflects good business acumen, quickness, and perhaps surprisingly, sexuality. Your mount has a refined, even texture that reflects your approach to communication.

COMPLEMENTARY READINGS

MERCURY MOUNT

SOLOMON RING
The ring around the base of your index finger is a mark of wisdom and leadership. Because both verbal and nonverbal communication are central to good leadership, your ability to convey information unambiguously is vital. A Solomon ring on only the dominant hand shows a sometimes reluctant leader, but one who is the best person for the job. A Solomon ring on only the passive hand shows an inner, prevailing need to take control.

FATE LINE
Your fate line has two starts, one from your life line, showing a possible link to a family profession, and one from the creative Luna mount. In your twenties, the two jobs, or parts of the job, come together but not for long. You seem more at ease with variety and settle in later years to successful self-employment.

VENUS MOUNT

◆ WELL-DEVELOPED

You are a "people" person, full of vitality, with a warm and loving nature. A large Venus mount shows a real zest for life, and can highlight virility. You need to be loved. The depth and size of the mount, with its firm and springy appearance, corresponds to inner resilience and reserves of energy. Larger than life, you have a capacity to work hard and play hard.

FINGERTIPS
The arch pattern on your index fingertip defines you as dedicated and loyal, with an overwhelming urge to provide security. The peacock's eye pattern on your ring fingertip shows you are protected from physical danger. On any other finger, this sign illustrates a degree of penetrating perception.

COMPLEMENTARY READINGS

INDEX FINGER
Your strong, firm index finger seems short in comparison to your middle and ring fingers, but as this is your passive hand, this feature represents your private, domestic self. Your family comes first.

HEALTH NOTE
A pattern of slashes across your heart line shows a possible potassium deficiency.

VENUS MOUNT

LUNA MOUNT

◆ WELL-DEVELOPED

You are creative and probably have a love of nature. Sensitive to moods, you are drawn to water. The bulging edge of your palm next to the Luna mount shows an interest in mysticism. A bulge so low that it almost overhangs the wrist shows psychic talent. This is the mount of the subconscious—if it is soft to the touch, you may be a dreamer who sees great things but never achieves them. However, in your case, the thumb, index finger, and Venus mount are all strong, showing that you are also an achiever.

COMPLEMENTARY READINGS

APOLLO MOUNT
A developed Apollo mount shows you have a sunny outlook and an attractive personality, but that you also seek the achievement of material prosperity and success.

ISLANDS
Island patterns on all your fingertips show you are sure to obtain success in anything you set out to achieve. Not a team player but a team leader, you are the one who sets the example.

LUNA MOUNT

CURVED LOOP
The curved loop coming into your Venus mount area shows an affinity with water.

THE MOUNTS

37

◆ WELL-DEVELOPED

You have a charismatic, magnetic personality. You are quick, perceptive, and charming, and are very likely a performer. You may utilize intuition as an aid to communication, and you are likely to have an interest in the spiritual and in mysticism. Neptune and Apollo mounts are both developed, showing that you work hard but play hard too.

HEAD LINE
Your independent head line starts on the Jupiter mount, running straight across the palm to the opposite edge. Your focus on business and leadership is reinforced by a strong and intensely directed work ethic.

COMPLEMENTARY READINGS

INDEX FINGER
Your index finger is very strong and thickly rooted, showing ambition with a strong business sense.

APOLLO MOUNT
With a full Apollo mount, you have a great sense of fun.

HEAD LINE
A depression, or blocking point, halfway along your head line reflects problems when you try to focus your thoughts. Given your business strengths, you find this immensely frustrating.

NEPTUNE MOUNT

MARS NEGATIVE MOUNT

◆ WELL-DEVELOPED

Also known as upper Mars, this mount is at the edge of the palm opposite the thumb, occupying the middle section. A high palm edge, like a thick rim, shows you are a principled person who works well under pressure. Your remarkable endurance is characterized by passive resistance and grim determination.

COMPLEMENTARY READINGS

RING
A ring on the middle finger shows a yearning for security, which may be provided by a stable and lasting partnership.

LITTLE FINGER
The second joint of your little finger is enlarged on the inside only, showing you to be sensual with an erotic frame of mind, qualities illustrated again by the lower phalanx being the largest.

FINGERS
The wide space between your index finger and your middle finger, and between your ring finger and little finger, reflects independence of thought and action.

THUMB
The long top phalanx of your thumb reveals strong willpower. Your thumb tip appears to have a flexible joint, but only the tip bends, indicating versatility and capability.

MARS NEGATIVE MOUNT

THE MOUNTS

◆ WELL-DEVELOPED

Also known as lower Mars, this mount is about physical courage and a fighting spirit. You are courageous and adventurous. A well-developed mount on a hand of a lower type could mean a very argumentative and confrontational person, even an aggressive one, but here it points to your love of a challenge. There is a line of courage crossing this mount, showing you to be a person who stands by whoever or whatever you believe in.

COMPLEMENTARY
READINGS

HEAD LINE
The independent head line start shows your independence of spirit. You are a risk taker.

MARS NEGATIVE MOUNT
Mars negative is also well-developed, showing moral courage, ethics, and integrity.

LUNA MOUNT
You have an investigative interest in the paranormal, shown by a developed lower Luna mount.

⌒ MARS POSITIVE MOUNT

THE MOUNTS

VENUS/NEPTUNE MOUNTS

1.10

◆ WELL-DEVELOPED

A "people" person, you know how to draw attention and admiration to yourself. You do your best work when dealing with the general public. Your developed Venus mount shows a warm, loving nature, vitality, and a zest for life. You need to be loved. With your developed Neptune mount, you have a charismatic personality. Quick, perceptive, and charming, you may be a performer, using intuition to aid communication.

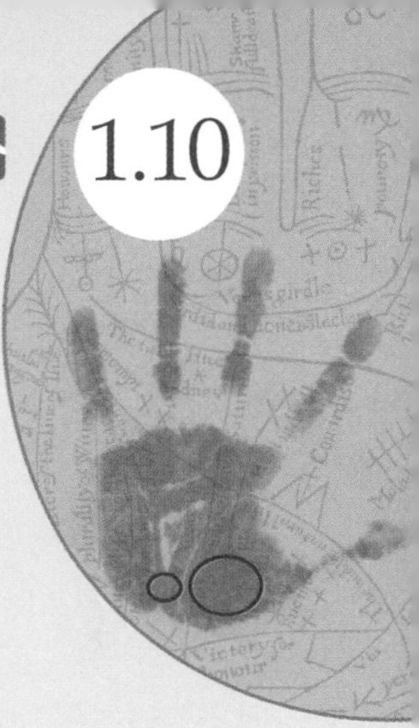

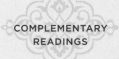

COMPLEMENTARY READINGS

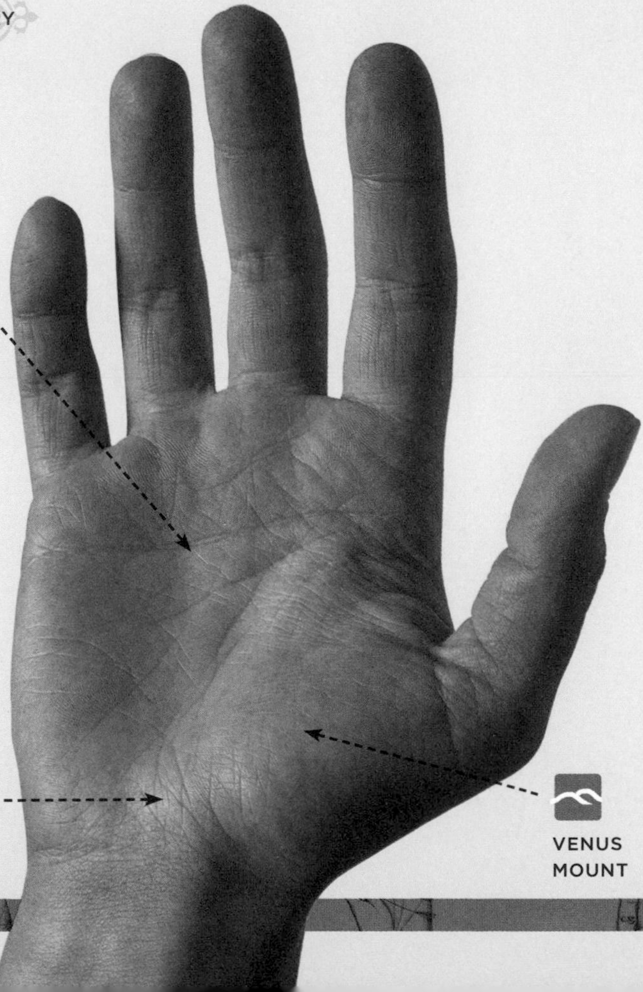

SIMIAN LINE
Your fused head and heart lines, defined as a simian line, display the intensity and focus you apply to anything you undertake. You are a person who always goes for it, and gets it.

NEPTUNE MOUNT

VENUS MOUNT

LIFE LINE

Will you have a long &
successful life?

LOCATION

The life line runs from between your thumb and index finger down toward your wrist. Birth is represented between the index finger and the thumb. Read the passage of life starting here and running around the ball of the thumb toward the wrist.

MEANING

The life line represents your general personality, life possibilities, the state of your health, and difficulties and successes as you navigate the maze of life. It may be short, straight, curved, or forked. Short life lines must never be assumed to denote a short life—on the contrary, the characteristics of a short line can mean a brand new life. Faintness or islands on the life line can indicate medical problems, trips to hospital, or other health-related issues. This section describes and illustrates many palms with variations to the life line.

Five Common Questions

◆ Will I emigrate?

◆ My "short" life line worries me; does it mean a short life?

◆ I have had so many traumas in my life. Will this current calm period continue?

◆ How will my health be in the future?

◆ Will I pass my exams?

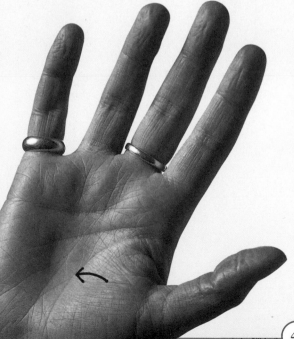

◮ LIFE LINE

- ◆ **RUNS CLOSE TO THUMB**
- ◆ **NARROW VENUS MOUNT**

You are shrewd and businesslike. Knowing how to keep a secret, you also keep issues and problems very much to yourself. With your life line starting high, you are a person who is single-minded and ambitious.

FRUSTRATION LINE
The lines crossing the tip of the thumb at right angles are frustration lines, suggesting that challenges to your willpower are likely to happen frequently.

COMPLEMENTARY READINGS

JUPITER MOUNT
Your Jupiter mount is well-developed, revealing ambition in the field of business.

TOP PHALANX
The top phalanx of your thumb is fairly long, showing strong willpower.

THUMB
The thumb, naturally held close, means that you tend to keep ideas, feelings, fears, and emotions in check, even when your partner wants to share them with you.

FATE LINE
The fate line appears to stop at the center of the palm, but it is actually a double fate line with a second part taking over from the first. Your job or career does not stop, but a second, more compulsive career becomes much more fulfilling.

◮ **LIFE LINE**

◆ **RUNS CLOSE TO THUMB**
◆ **NARROW VENUS MOUNT**

You are shrewd and businesslike. Inclined to be introverted, you know how to keep a secret, but also keep problems and feelings to yourself. Your life line has a number of lines crossing it at right angles. Signifying dramatic incidents, these trauma lines seem to cease around the age of thirty. Around the late forties, you have a line going to the fate line and back to the life line, which may mean a major relocation, followed by a return home.

COMPLEMENTARY READINGS

LIFE LINE ⋀⋀

STAR
The star on the Apollo mount is a clear sign of fame and fortune.

ISLANDS
Some of your fingers show an island pattern, a sign of concentration and focus that signifies success.

TEACHER'S SQUARE
The teacher's square, visible on the Jupiter mount, shows your ability to convey information effectively. It does not necessarily mean that your career is in teaching.

FATE LINE
Your fate line starts with a fork, which usually indicates vocational study as well as a job. The fork is the merging of the two, with the stronger line showing it is a good career decision.

HEAD LINE
Your head line ends firmly in the Luna mount, a creative and artistic area.

⋀ LIFE LINE

◆ RUNS WIDE AROUND THE THUMB
◆ WELL-DEVELOPED VENUS MOUNT

You are a "people" person with a wide circle of friends. Your life line shows an emigration around middle age. As you are right-handed and this is your left hand, your parents have moved from their country of birth. Two trauma lines cross your life line at right angles, signifying two significant events between the ages of twenty and thirty. Your life line continues straight and deep, reflecting a clear path in life with few serious health issues.

COMPLEMENTARY READINGS

FINGERS
The middle fingers linked together show that you tend to feel guilt in pleasure.

GIRDLE OF VENUS
The partial girdle of Venus adds a sensual and sensitive side to your personality. If the marking is not reflected in your dominant hand, this part of your nature is suppressed.

SOLOMON RING
You have the start and end of a Solomon ring, showing your desire to take over and organize, particularly at work.

⋀ LIFE LINE

MARS LINE
The Mars line, running inside your life line close to the thumb, protects you like a guardian angel.

FATE LINE
Your fate line is strong and determined, indicating that you will continue a career beyond retirement age.

LIFE LINE

LIFE LINE ᛗᛗ

◆ **RUNS WIDE AROUND THE THUMB**
◆ **WELL-DEVELOPED VENUS MOUNT**

You are a "people" person, with a wide circle of friends.
Your life line runs straight and clear for most of its length,
but becomes fainter with a small fork at around the age
of sixty. This looks like a health problem with the lower
back. The fork is likely to represent a move, perhaps to an
apartment or bungalow. Trauma lines from the teens to the
thirties have little effect on the strength of your life line.
You are a remarkably resilient person.

**COMPLEMENTARY
READINGS**

ᛗᛗ **LIFE LINE**

**LOOP OF
VOCATION**
Between your
two middle
fingers, the loop
of vocation
displays your
commitment to
helping people.

**MARS POSITIVE
MOUNT**
A shallow area in the Mars
positive mount shows that
you have brilliant personnel
skills, with the ability to
assess people quickly
and accurately.

**LOOP OF
HUMOR**
Between your
ring and little
fingers, the
loop of humor
reveals a dry
sense of humor.

THUMB TIP
Your thumb tip
has a flattened
pad, showing
sensitivity to moods.
You instinctively
know how to make
someone happy or sad.

LIFE LINE

ᴍ LIFE LINE

◆ **APPEARS TO BE SHORT**
◆ **APPEARS TO BE BROKEN**

There is often a faint line connecting a short life line to the fate line. Usually this means emigration, with the distance from the life line to the fate line representing the distance traveled. Your life line links faintly to your fate line around the age of fifty-five, showing that your career will be the likely cause of your move. With a high start close to your thumb, your life line shows that you are an ambitious go-getter who plays your cards close to the chest.

COMPLEMENTARY READINGS

SUCCESS LINE
The success line reflecting the higher part of your fate line emphasizes that your career move will be a success.

ᴍ LIFE LINE

LOWER PHALANX
The short lower phalanx of your little finger reveals a strong desire to belong.

VENUS MOUNT
Your Venus mount is fairly full and rounded, showing vitality for life and love.

FATE LINE
Upward branches on your fate line mean a lot of job opportunities. Settling around the age of fifty-five and actually doubling, your fate line shows you will have two careers for a number of years.

THUMB
Your thumb is fairly rigid, indicating rigidly held ideas.

PALM
The square, solid palm and shortish fingers reveal you to be naturally cautious.

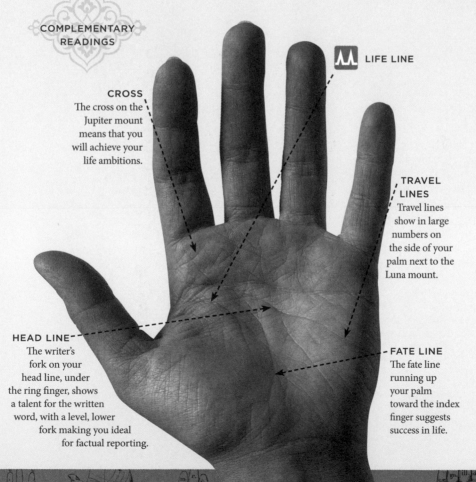

LIFE LINE

- ◆ **APPEARS TO BE SHORT**
- ◆ **APPEARS TO BE BROKEN**

Your life line is chained and crossed in the early stages, showing problems and your difficulty in coming to terms with them. In the early twenties, there is a long line linking the life line to the fate line. In the dominant hand, this is likely to mean emigration, with the distance from the life line to the fate line representing the distance traveled. Beneath the start of your life line is just the start of a double life line, which may indicate a missed opportunity.

COMPLEMENTARY READINGS

LIFE LINE

CROSS
The cross on the Jupiter mount means that you will achieve your life ambitions.

TRAVEL LINES
Travel lines show in large numbers on the side of your palm next to the Luna mount.

HEAD LINE
The writer's fork on your head line, under the ring finger, shows a talent for the written word, with a level, lower fork making you ideal for factual reporting.

FATE LINE
The fate line running up your palm toward the index finger suggests success in life.

LIFE LINE

♙ LIFE LINE

◆ **SHORT**
◆ **HAS BREAK IN IT**

With a break in the life line, you usually see a faint line connecting the life line to the fate line. This often signals emigration, with the distance from your life line to your fate line giving an idea of the distance traveled. Sometimes a break represents a radical change of circumstances and environment. You may, for example, suddenly receive a large fortune.

FAMILY RINGS
You have family rings on your little finger and your thumb. The doubling on your thumb suggests a second family home and an inheritance— this could be the early change of circumstances shown by the break in your life line.

COMPLEMENTARY READINGS

FATE LINE
A double start from the Luna mount reveals success, either through a family connection or personal ability.

♙ **LIFE LINE**

SUCCESS LINE
Starting early and running beside your doubled fate line, your success line shows your very promising career prospects.

ANGLE OF TIMING
The angle of your thumb where it meets your hand shows good timing, with respect to career, business, or music. You may be a proficient musician.

◆ **DOUBLE**
◆ **FULL OR PARTIAL**

A double life line denotes your potential to lead a double life, one ordinary and the other more exciting. Many show-business personalities have this feature. Your second line, running inside the main life line, very deep and close to the thumb, is only developed into your early twenties, indicating that you are not exploiting this second facet of your life. Its depth, however, shows that this second life opportunity is not going to go away.

COMPLEMENTARY READINGS

HEALTH NOTE
Exhaustion lines run up your fingers into several fingertips, showing that you lack a natural safety valve to tell you when to take a break.

𝗠 LIFE LINE

HEAD LINE
Your head line starts high, independently of your life line, showing you to be an adventurous, impulsive, and ambitious risk taker. You are highly motivated and capable of great achievement.

THUMB
With a long lower phalanx cut around with many resistance rings, you are a very logical, yet highly intuitive person, capable of great perception and foresight.

⋀ LIFE LINE

◆ **FULL**
◆ **FORKED END**

After a tough decision in your early to middle fifties, you will emigrate or make a major life change. The clarity and depth of the branch shows your decision to be a good one. The fork connects to the fate line, showing that your potential change of country will probably be associated with career progression or advancement. Latticework tying the start of the life line to the head line denotes bouts of both confidence and hesitancy.

ISLAND
The island pattern on your index fingertip is usually a sign of success. You will achieve this by being single-minded and by working independently.

COMPLEMENTARY READINGS

JUPITER MOUNT
Both your index finger and Jupiter mount are dominant, revealing a strongly ambitious individual.

⋀ **LIFE LINE**

CROSS
A cross on your Apollo mount, straddling the success line, suggests financial problems. These will, however, be temporary, as shown by the strength of the success line after the cross.

MARS LINE
Your Mars line, running inside the life line close to your thumb, is adjacent to the fork in the life line, providing protection during what could be a difficult period.

BUSINESS LINE
This line, branching from your fate line toward your Mercury mount and little finger, indicates the blossoming of strong business links for you.

◆ **FULL**
◆ **FORKED END**

After a tough decision in your sixties, you will emigrate or make a major life change. Both branches of the fork are deep and clear, showing a strong possibility that you will have two very different homes and share time between them.

COMPLEMENTARY READINGS

HEAD LINE
A sharply dipping head line, together with a short top thumb phalanx, hold you back, undermining the great achievements of which you are capable.

FINGERS
The thick lower phalanxes reveal that you value material wealth.

LIFE LINE

FATE LINE
Starting on the Luna mount, your fate line reveals capability. Coupled with a thickset index finger, this means you are very ambitious.

HEALTH NOTE
Double health lines crossing the hand from the middle of the wrist to the little finger show that you need to, and do, take extra care with your health.

VENUS MOUNT
Your padded mount dominates the rest of your palm, speaking volumes about your need for creature comforts.

LIFE LINE

⋀ LIFE LINE

◆ ENDS TUCKED UNDER BALL OF THUMB

You may be well-traveled, but you always love to return home, and you need to make wherever you are feel like home. Your head line, starting connected to your life line, reinforces a strong attachment to home, and indicates a high degree of sensitivity to the opinions of others. If possible, avoid people who are critical. With an early branch to the Jupiter mount and a branch from the life line to the little finger, you have strong ambition and are especially well-placed for financial success.

COMPLEMENTARY
READINGS

FATE LINE
Starting on the Luna mount, your fate line indicates creative talent. You must use it or it will consume you.

FAMILY RINGS
Family rings around the base of the thumb and little finger reflect the importance of family ties.

ARTISTIC FLAIR
The curving at the edge of the palm away from the thumb shows artistic flair.

LIFE LINE ⋀

◆ ENDS SWEEPING AWAY FROM THUMB

You are an adventurous person who enjoys roaming far and wide. Early connecting lines between your life and head lines show both high confidence and self-doubt. As your abilities are confirmed, these branches and anxieties will fade. You have great influence in your personal life and your career, shown by the influence lines in your thirties crossing both the life and fate lines. The lines grow stronger, confirming that your influence has been an asset.

COMPLEMENTARY READINGS

FAMILY RINGS

Family rings around both the thumb and little finger show the importance you place on home and family. A person who probably travels a great deal for work, you have a greater appreciation of home on your return.

ATTACHMENT LINE

Your attachment line breaks but rejoins. If your marriage or partnership suffers an actual separation, it will not last long.

VIA LASCIVIA

Via lascivia cutting low across the palm on the side opposite to the thumb was historically thought to denote an alcoholic or a drug user. Today, the opposite is true— it shows that you have a high degree of sensitivity, or even allergy, to alcohol and/or drugs of any type.

 LIFE LINE

LIFE LINE

∧∧ LIFE LINE

◆ STARTS HIGH

You are an ambitious and single-minded individual with a very strong desire to succeed in life. Although crossed lines and chains show early problems, your life line happily becomes clearer and stronger as it proceeds. The life line running close around the thumb, coupled with the thumb naturally held close to the hand, reveal that you are cautious and like control.

SUCCESS LINE
Mirroring your fate line for most of its length, your success line shows success throughout your career, through recognition, financial reward, or promotion. Later in life, the fate and success lines branch, signifying successful self-employment or running of a business.

COMPLEMENTARY READINGS

FATE AND HEAD LINES
These lines resemble those of a model on international assignments.

FATE LINE
Starting forked, your fate line becomes one strong, flexible line. You start with two careers, gaining success from combining your talents but remaining flexible.

∧∧ LIFE LINE

LIFE LINE

- ◆ **STARTS LOW**
- ◆ **CLOSER TO THE THUMB**

You are a content and accepting person, who does not like to cause trouble. Your life line sweeps wide, encompassing a wide circle of family and friends. The fact that the life line starts connected to the head line shows that you enjoy the company and good opinion of others but are not overconcerned. Your hand contains many signs of a natural healer.

COMPLEMENTARY READINGS

HEALING STRIATA
Three short lines on the Mercury mount, the healing striata, reveal that you have a talent for putting people at ease. The lines often refer to alternative medicine.

SYMPATHY/ EMPATHY LINES
Sympathy/empathy lines crossing the Jupiter mount show that you care, possibly too deeply. One line means you are ideally suited to the healing and caring professions; multiple lines mean you feel the pain of others.

LIFE LINE

MERCURY LINE
The double health line coming from the Neptune mount toward your little finger is the Mercury line, which reveals your ability to communicate in a healing way.

VENUS MOUNT
Your full Venus mount reflects your vitality and general sociability.

⋀⋀ LIFE LINE

◆ **PASSIVE**

◆ **DIFFERENT FROM DOMINANT**

There are fundamental differences between your left, passive palm and your right, dominant palm with its double life line. The second, inner life line is undeveloped on your passive hand, indicating a need for security. Also not present in this hand is a break in your life line. The small part of the double life line that is present is covered with trauma lines, showing that you have overcome a great deal to get to your position in life.

INDEX FINGER
A capable and confident person (long index and ring fingers), your slightly bent index finger reveals you to be a little unsure of yourself.

COMPLEMENTARY READINGS

SOLOMON RING
Absent from the dominant hand, this ring around the base of the index finger shows wisdom, ambition, and leadership, felt as an inner force driving you onward.

LIFE LINE ⋀⋀

NO CURVED LOOP
The absence of a curved loop on your passive hand suggests that your affinity for water is more of a physical outlet.

HEAD LINE
Your head line does not start from inside your life line. When you display temper, your inner self does not feel it and is possibly confused by it.

LIFE LINE

LIFE LINE 2.16

- ◆ **DOMINANT**
- ◆ **DOUBLE**
- ◆ **FULL OR PARTIAL**

Your double life line shows you lead a double life, part mundane and part exciting. This is often present on the hands of actors. A break in the life line in your early twenties shows a time of turmoil, with the overlap representing the healing of a broken life. This break comes after a number of trauma lines, indicating difficult incidents. Life settles down after your early twenties.

COMPLEMENTARY READINGS

FATE LINE
An early start points to early success and, starting from the Luna mount, shows you excelling in the public arena. You are suited to a career in politics.

HEAD LINE
Starting just inside the life line, your head line could indicate a belligerent and irascible temper. This is not a sign of willful aggression—you simply tend to attack as the best form of defense.

CURVED LOOP
A curved loop pattern, below your head line into the Luna mount, shows your strong affinity for water. You may have a home near the sea or a sporting interest involving water. However expressed, water in its many forms makes you come alive.

LIFE LINE

HEART LINE

Who do you love?

LOCATION

The heart line runs under and closest to the fingers. Read it from the edge of the palm as it runs toward the index finger. Birth is shown at the start of the line between the index finger and thumb, with life stretching across the palm.

MEANING

The heart line represents both the physical heart, your feelings, and emotional attitude. All your partnerships, terminated relationships, and love affairs show up on the heart line, as well as experiences involving pain, hurt, and despair. The partners you attract and those you prefer may not be the same ones—if the heart line is different on each hand, you may be attracting a person who is far from your ideal partner. This section describes and illustrates many palms with variations to the heart line.

✦ Five Common Questions ✦

- ◆ Did I choose the right partner?

- ◆ Will I meet my soul mate?

- ◆ In later life, will I be as happy and content with my partner as I am right now?

- ◆ My working life seems to be more important than my love life; will this always be the case?

- ◆ Why do I seem to attract the wrong sort of person?

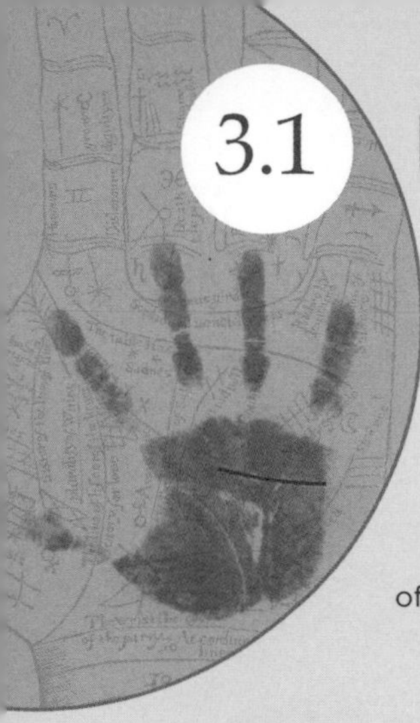

- ◆ **SHORT**
- ◆ **STRAIGHT**
- ◆ **ENDS UNDER MIDDLE FINGER**

Love and romance are important to you but intimacy is possible without love. An intellectually like-minded partner is essential, given your straight heart line. The end of your heart line branching back toward your head line suggests that your head rules your heart—you stand a good chance of becoming a workaholic.

COMPLEMENTARY
READINGS

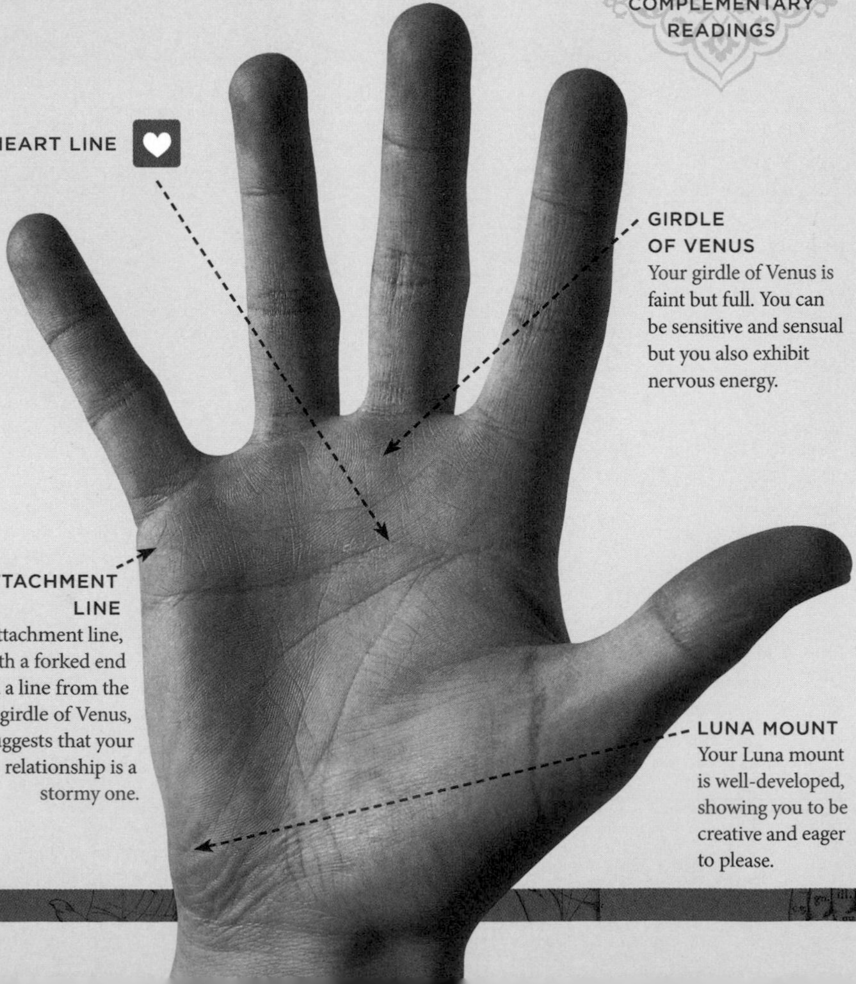

HEART LINE ♥

GIRDLE OF VENUS
Your girdle of Venus is faint but full. You can be sensitive and sensual but you also exhibit nervous energy.

ATTACHMENT LINE
The attachment line, with a forked end and a line from the girdle of Venus, suggests that your relationship is a stormy one.

LUNA MOUNT
Your Luna mount is well-developed, showing you to be creative and eager to please.

HEART LINE

HEART LINE ♥

◆ SHORT
◆ STRAIGHT
◆ ENDS UNDER MIDDLE FINGER

You have a shrewd, remote, almost businesslike approach to relationships. Although love and romance are important to you, intimacy is possible without love. With your straight heart line, an intellectually like-minded partner is essential.

COMPLEMENTARY READINGS

HEAD LINE
Your head line springs from your Jupiter mount, showing that drive and aggression easily color your thinking. Starting independently of your life line, it reveals that, as a child, you seek independence, and have a tendency to be impulsive. In maturity, you are a risk taker, and have spectacular failures and successes.

STARS
Stars on both your Apollo and Saturn mounts show you achieving excellence and a hard-earned fortune.

ATTACHMENT LINE
The forked end may indicate a parting of the ways with your partner, or may mean that, although you live together, you lead very separate lives.

SUCCESS LINE
The line from your success line toward your little finger is known as the business line. Your career is heavily dependent on insight and inspiration for its prosperity.

♥ **HEART LINE**

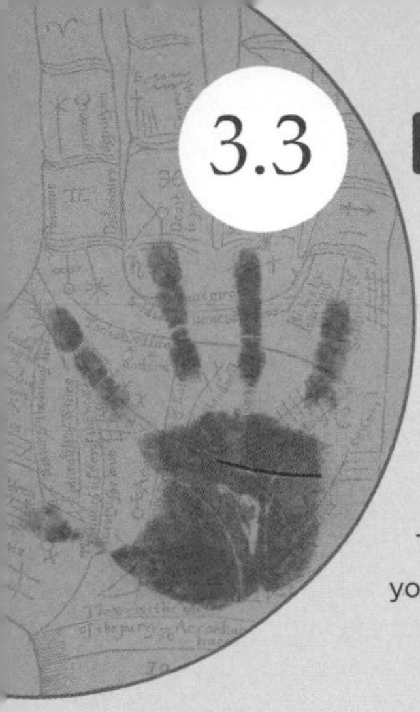

♥ HEART LINE

◆ **LONG**
◆ **STRAIGHT**
◆ **ENDS UNDER INDEX FINGER**

You have a strong sense of purpose; you may be a workaholic. This tendency is supported by a horizontal branch from the life line to the heart line. A line running to the index finger from the same point highlights ambition and success. The line slanting slightly toward the Jupiter mount shows that you have a romantic side that softens the effect.

COMPLEMENTARY READINGS

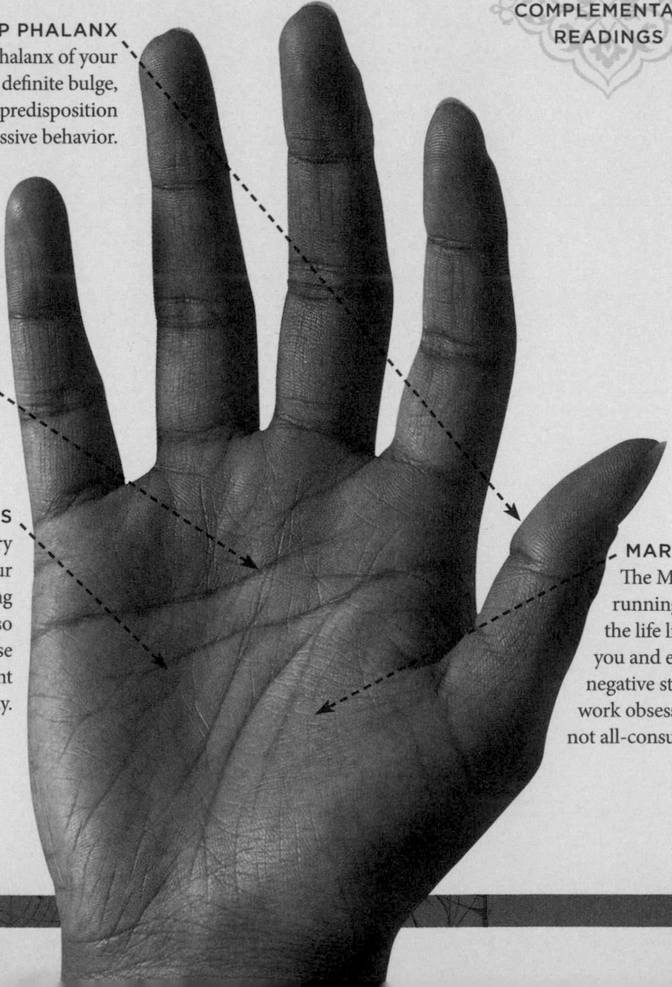

TOP PHALANX
The top phalanx of your thumb has a definite bulge, showing your predisposition toward obsessive behavior.

HEART LINE ♥

STRESS LINES
Stress lines are very apparent on your palm, revealing overwork. It is also possible that these lines could represent too much play.

MARS LINE
The Mars line running inside the life line protects you and ensures that negative stress and work obsession are not all-consuming.

HEART LINE ♥

◆ **ENDS UNDER INDEX FINGER**
◆ **ENDS ON JUPITER MOUNT**

This feminine line, found on the hands of both sexes, is both romantic and indicative of emotional vulnerability. Your heart line ends with a branch flicking sharply backward. Known as a kinky flick, this simply means that you have an adventurous attitude in relationships. The straightness of the line shows that romance is important to you, but you are not considered a romantic.

COMPLEMENTARY READINGS

GIRDLE OF VENUS
A partial girdle of Venus reflects your earthy sensuality.

HEAD LINE
Your long, straight head line shows a practical mentality, with a factual and scientific approach to schemes and ideas. You are ideally suited to a career in information technology, business, or commerce.

HEART LINE ♥

SOLOMON RING
The combination of a partial Solomon ring and a strong index finger shows that you push to take the lead in business dealings.

HEART LINE

♥ HEART LINE

◆ ENDS BETWEEN INDEX AND MIDDLE FINGERS

This masculine line is a dominant, demanding line. You are a confirmed sensualist, but the branch toward the Jupiter mount shows that you are also capable of romance. In traditional palmistry, the many branches mean that you date or have dated a lot, with each line representing a partner. Today, however, it is considered just as likely that you have just one partner, with the many branches signifying the many different demands you make of him or her. If one person meets all your needs, it will be a sensational partnership.

COMPLEMENTARY
READINGS

APOLLO MOUNT
Your developed Apollo mount suggests an appreciation of money and a strong sense of fun. People are naturally drawn to you.

**FRUSTRATION
LINES**
Frustration lines running across your little finger indicate that you have communication difficulties.

**GIRDLE
OF VENUS**
A partial girdle of Venus reflects an earthy sensuality and a certain sensitivity.

HEART LINE ♥

HEART LINE ♥

◆ ENDS BETWEEN INDEX AND MIDDLE FINGERS

You love strongly and deeply, but you express love more with actions than words. The end of your heart line tends toward the base of your index finger, which may show your idealism about partners. You strike a good balance between being too idealistic and too sexual. The many heart line branches either mean a lot of dating, or dating one person but demanding different things from the relationship almost daily.

COMPLEMENTARY READINGS

TOP PHALANXES
Long top phalanxes on your fingers show you are an action person who likes to get on with things. In love, you tend to rush in without fully thinking it through.

♥ **HEART LINE**

APOLLO MOUNT
Your well-developed Apollo mount indicates you are open and friendly and attract a lot of people.

VENUS MOUNT
A full, rounded Venus mount reflects a lovely, warm love life, expressive of healthy physical desires.

HEART LINE

♥ HEART LINE

◆ **FORKED END**
◆ **TRIDENT END**

Filled with warmth, idealism, and passion, you have a sensible approach to relationships. The branch of the fork running between the index and middle fingers shows, at its fullest extent, an out-and-out sensualist, but your line stops short of this extreme. The second branch, running straight across your palm, shows a workaholic tendency, but again this line stops short, revealing your fairly serious outlook on relationships.

COMPLEMENTARY
READINGS

HEART LINE ♥

VENUS MOUNT
Your full mount shows vitality, virility, and sexuality and, as the largest mount of your hand, is the most dominant. These principles are your driving forces.

HEALTH NOTE
The top bracelet on your wrist is arched upward, pointing to a weakness in the genital/urinary area. Infections are possible, in both men and women.

THUMB
The top phalanx represents willpower. Your short phalanx denotes a lack of willpower, which, combined with your sensual inquisitiveness and focus on vitality and sexuality, makes you susceptible to temptation. This could give you problems.

HEART LINE ♥

◆ STRONG
◆ CLEAR

You have a clear, straightforward approach to partnerships. A very wide, very deep line suggests a love life that is stuck in a rut. A heart line ending both in the area of the index finger, and between the index and middle fingers, indicates that you have a mixed approach to love and are generally a well-balanced, loving, sensuous, and romantic person.

COMPLEMENTARY READINGS

♥ HEART LINE

GIRDLE OF VENUS
The girdle of Venus shows the sensual side of your nature.

LEGACY LINE
Springing from an influence line inside the life line, you have a legacy line that runs to the success line. Support and help from your family will bring about your success.

FATE LINE
Your fate line shows you suffering a career setback early in life. Flexibility later in your career gives you renewed strength.

VENUS MOUNT
Your Venus mount is well-developed, showing good vitality, sexuality, and libido. Although you will not, of course, feel sexy all the time, you have a definite overall loving outlook.

HEART LINE

♥ HEART LINE

◆ MANY BRANCHES

Either you make diverse demands on your partner on an almost daily basis, or you have dated a great deal. If there has been just one partner, your partnership is a very special one to have stood the test of time and your demands. Ending around the Jupiter mount, your heart line reveals your tendency toward the romantic. The many end branches coming down to the head line indicate that your thoughtfulness is appreciated.

MARS LINE
The Mars line, the protection and fight back line, is present inside your life line closest to the thumb. You approach any health difficulties with a practical "get on with it" attitude.

COMPLEMENTARY READINGS

THUMB
The thumb held close does not look natural. Perhaps lessons you have learned in life have resulted in keeping problems and feelings to yourself.

HEART LINE ♥

HEALTH NOTE
The extra pattern of dashes over your heart line may point to a potassium deficiency.

INTUITION LINES
Intuition lines are abundant in the creative and imaginative Luna mount area. You are probably very good at second-guessing.

INTUITION RINGS
The many rings crossing the lower phalanx of your thumb are known as intuition rings.

HEART LINE ♥

◆ DOUBLE
◆ PARALLEL ANYWHERE

Twice the line means twice the heart. An attractive and loving person, you have a great capacity for love. Your heart line doubles at its end, with the lower, continuous line short and straight, indicating your potential both to love deeply and your susceptibility to fleeting affairs. The upper line ends between your index and middle fingers, which means that the sensual side of your relationships is strongly highlighted.

COMPLEMENTARY READINGS

FAMILY RINGS
Rings at the base of your thumb and little finger look like chains with fairly large links, suggesting that you are close to your family.

ATTACHMENT LINES
Two lines running parallel and close denote two relationships, possibly overlapping. The second line is fainter, showing that a second, conflicting relationship could be avoided if necessary. The second attachment line would be likely to fade over time and even disappear.

THUMB
Your well-developed top phalanx shows potential for obsessive behavior.

HEART LINE ♥

♥ HEART LINE

◆ **PASSIVE**

◆ **DIFFERENT FROM DOMINANT**

There are fundamental differences between your left, passive palm and your right, dominant palm. On the dominant hand, the passive heart line has a fork running between the fingers, showing sensuality. The second branch runs onto the Jupiter mount but not the finger, showing your inner self to be romantic. The third branch does not appear, indicating that your outward self attracts a different type of person than your inner self desires.

APOLLO MOUNT
Some success is apparent from your success line, but the star on the mount is absent. Fame and fortune could have passed you by had you not made changes to your life.

COMPLEMENTARY READINGS

HEAD LINE
This passive hand has a sharply dipping head line. This may show inner depression with some dark moods that do not show in your outer life. This line also reflects the fact that you have highly creative and complex ideas.

ATTACHMENT LINE
Parallel relationship lines mean simultaneous relationships. As these are not present in your dominant hand, the potential for a second, simultaneous relationship will not be realized.

TRAVEL LINES
A number of travel lines are present, but the significant business connection is absent.

HEART LINE ♥

HEART LINE ♥

◆ DOMINANT
◆ ENDS ON INDEX FINGER

You have an idealistic approach to relationships. Unless blessed with a truly perfect partner, you are an emotionally vulnerable individual. Your heart line has a faint fork running between the fingers, signifying sensuality. The branch leading to your index finger does not travel too far up the finger, revealing curbed idealism. However, the third branch traveling across your hand reflects a workaholic with idealistic tendencies.

COMPLEMENTARY READINGS

HEART LINE ♥

GIRDLE OF VENUS
A full girdle of Venus shows your sensitivity, compassion, and sensuality. Along with the idealistic aspects of the heart line and stress markings across the hand, the full girdle indicates a degree of nervousness and jumpiness in your character.

FATE LINE
Running toward the Jupiter mount, your fate line shows a strong sense of purpose. You are proud and ambitious. There are a number of breaks on the line, but each overlaps, showing your unique skills and versatility.

TRAVEL LINES
A number of significant journeys are represented on the outer edge of your palm. One particular line meets the success line, indicating a successful business link with a contact in another country or with a foreign person in your own country.

STAR
A star on your Apollo mount signals fame and fortune in the future, earned through hard effort.

HEAD LINE

Are you intellectually
superior?

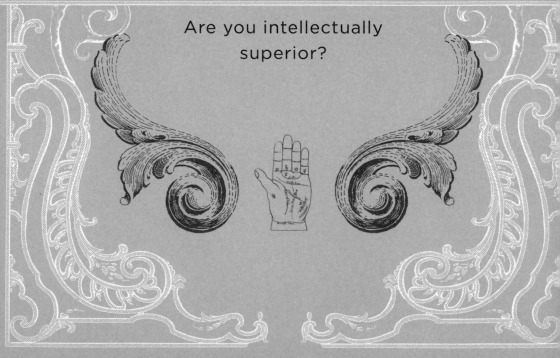

LOCATION

The head line starts between the index finger and the thumb, above the life line, and usually below the end of the heart line. Birth is represented between the index finger and the thumb. Read the passage of life starting here and running across the palm to the edge away from the thumb.

MEANING

The head line represents both the physical head and breadth of intellect and understanding. A sharply dipping line can give a negative aspect to an individual's outlook, but also speaks volumes in terms of potential genius. This section describes and illustrates many palms with variations to the head line.

Five Common Questions

- ◆ What type of career suits me best?
- ◆ Do I have a natural talent as a writer?
- ◆ Am I holding myself back from achieving more?
- ◆ Is ambition part of my nature?
- ◆ Why is it that study seems easier for me than for others?

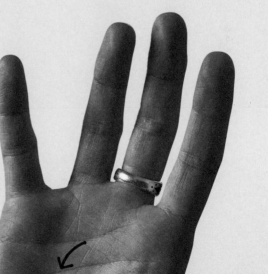

◨ HEAD LINE

- ◆ **SHORT**
- ◆ **STRAIGHT**
- ◆ **ENDS UNDER MIDDLE FINGER**

Perhaps an initiator, you have a desire for security. You are probably a very practical person, good at solving problems. This line is also often found on specialists, such as doctoral students. The outer angle of your lower thumb joint, known as the angle of dexterity, is fairly pronounced, showing both manual and mental dexterity.

LOOP OF HUMOR
The loop of humor, between the ring finger and little finger, is well-defined, showing your good, rich sense of fun.

COMPLEMENTARY READINGS

HEART LINE
Your short heart line means that you have a very direct approach to sex and relationships, although the curve shows there is also room for hearts, flowers, and romance.

ATTACHMENT LINE
The attachment line has a faint forked end. There is a strong chance that you will be able to patch up any relationship or marriage difficulties.

HEAD LINE

VENUS MOUNT
A full, rounded Venus mount denotes a lovely, warm love life expressing healthy physical desires. Open and friendly, you attract a lot of people with your witty and charming personality.

- ◆ **LONG**
- ◆ **STRAIGHT**
- ◆ **ENDS UNDER RING OR MIDDLE FINGER**

You have a practical mentality and are ideally suited to science, technology, and business. Known as a Sydney line, this head line suggests the fierce intensity and focus associated with the simian line. Your fate line, directed to the index finger, points to a strong managerial focus to your career. You have a good chance of success in this field, but at a price—you have many stress lines.

COMPLEMENTARY READINGS

EXHAUSTION LINES
The well-defined exhaustion lines running up your fingers extend into the fingertips, meaning you have trouble knowing when to stop. Very obvious when you run a fingernail lightly across your fingers from left to right, these lines show that your inner reserves are being severely depleted. Take a break.

RING
The ring on your middle finger shows an inner yearning for security.

STRESS LINES
Many negative stress lines are a sign of an achievement-oriented person.

HEAD LINE

LOWER PHALANX
The lower phalanx of your thumb is long, showing good logic. Here, the many crossing lines show a high level of almost psychic intuition.

TOP PHALANX
The long top phalanx of your thumb shows strong willpower, but the crossing lines demonstrate your need to bend a little.

HEAD LINE

☐ HEAD LINE

◆ **LONG**
◆ **CURVES DOWNWARD**

The head line ends on the Luna mount, indicating a creative and artistic talent. Your head line starts independently of your life line, showing independence from an early age. You are an adventurous risk taker. The latticework of lines connecting the start of your head line to your life line reveals bursts of confidence alternating with withdrawals into self-doubt. These lines appear fairly faint, suggesting that you are overcoming your self-doubt.

ISLANDS
The island patterns on the fingertips of your index and ring fingers signify success, both in the domain of business and ambition and in the domain of fun and pleasure.

COMPLEMENTARY READINGS

SUCCESS LINE
Your success line comes into its own on your Apollo mount, clearly showing public recognition. Considering your fate line, real recognition and satisfaction will probably not come solely from a conventional job.

☐ **HEAD LINE**

WHORL
A palmar ridge whorl, such as this one on your Luna mount, shows a special gift or talent. It can also signal a heartfelt desire to fulfill yourself creatively. Write that novel or paint that masterpiece.

FATE LINE
Your career has an uncertain start, settling into job satisfaction in your twenties. A period of self-employment in your late forties or fifties provides some success.

◆ LONG
◆ SHARPLY DIPPING

You are imaginative with melancholic tendencies if suppressed. This is the thin line between genius and madness. Your curved head line running deep into the Luna mount shows that you are not entirely materialistic in your ideas. This line reveals that you have the qualities needed for translating, public speaking, or writing. Trusting feelings is second nature to you, and behavior perceived by others as irrational often gets surprising results.

COMPLEMENTARY READINGS

HEAD LINE 🙂

AMBITION LINE
The short line running from your life line to your Jupiter mount is known as an ambition line, and shows that you will achieve your ambitions. These are likely to be academic ambitions, such as passing an examination.

LITTLE FINGER
Your little finger stands apart, denoting independence of thought. You will probably enter a creative or artistic profession or be the leader of an organization.

HEALTH NOTE
A particularly low freckle on your hand could point to a copper deficiency, especially if it has not always been there.

HEAD LINE

HEAD LINE

◆ STARTS CONNECTED TO LIFE LINE

You are often more cautious and careful than is warranted, tending to measure yourself by what others think of you. Despite being straight and strong, your head line remains connected to your life line for some distance, showing a lack of confidence or self-assurance. You should generally try to avoid negative and overcritical people. Sufficient talent and strong qualities will eventually help to reassure you, but your major achievements are often the result of wanting to prove yourself over and over again.

GIRDLE OF VENUS
The girdle of Venus shows a strong possibility that you are overemotional.

COMPLEMENTARY READINGS

HEAD LINE

FATE LINE
Your fate line starts very close to your life line. Together with the tied head and life lines, this shows your strong link to family members and their opinions, or suggests that you will do well in a family profession.

MARS LINE
Your Mars line, the guardian angel line, shows that you are able to spring back and pick up the pieces when life gets you down.

LOWER PHALANX
The lower phalanx of your thumb is long, indicating that you have a logical nature.

TOP PHALANX
The long top phalanx of your thumb shows willpower to help you overcome any feelings of inadequacy.

◆ START COMPLETELY SEPARATE FROM LIFE LINE

You have always been strongly independent, even in childhood. Likely to be an adventurous and impulsive risk taker, you may inspire criticism for being too outspoken. Your unpredictable approach to projects can sometimes work spectacularly and at other times can be your undoing. The combination of your short top thumb phalanx, denoting low willpower, and your very long ring finger indicates your susceptibility to excessive gambling. It is worth noting that it is not just money that can be gambled.

COMPLEMENTARY READINGS

HEAD LINE

ISLAND
An island fingerprint pattern on your index finger is a good sign of success, but this is more likely to be achieved working alone than as part of a team.

VIA LASCIVIA
Once interpreted as a lascivious, overindulgent marking, via lascivia is more correctly interpreted today as a sign of allergies or of sensitivity to alcohol or painkillers, even in the smallest quantities.

HEAD LINE
The upward fork on your head line points to strong business knowledge and acumen, which, together with a strong index finger, could be your saving grace.

HEAD LINE

81

HEAD LINE

◆ **STARTS HIGH**
◆ **CLOSER TO INDEX FINGER THAN THUMB**

Highly motivated and capable of great achievements, you are by nature ambitious. The start of your head line is separate from your life line, denoting your independence. You know your own mind and are also potentially a risk taker. The strong, deep, and clear head line shows clarity of thought applied in a straightforward and logical way.

ARCH
An arch fingerprint pattern on the index finger shows a strong sense of wanting to protect and secure everyone and everything around you. This urge is likely to be an active part of your personality.

COMPLEMENTARY READINGS

LOOP OF HUMOR
Though you are charming and friendly, the combination of a loop of humor between the ring and little fingers, and a developed Venus mount, makes you positively magnetic.

HEAD LINE

HEART LINE
Ending on the index finger, your heart line shows a tendency to idealize partnerships. This is a possible reason for the number of negative stress lines on your palm.

TOP PHALANX
The top phalanx of your thumb reveals a lot of willpower, with the backward flex showing a wide circle of friends.

HEAD LINE

82

◆ STARTS LOW
◆ CLOSER TO THUMB THAN INDEX FINGER

A head line very close to the thumb indicates that you may have low self-esteem and a strong temper. Misunderstood, you tend to use attack as the best form of defense. Although your life line starts low, showing calm and acceptance, your long head line, known as a Sydney line, reflects your fiery intensity, focus, and determination, very much like a simian line. A line of courage cuts across the palm from just above the thumb.

COMPLEMENTARY READINGS

HEAD LINE ◖

FATE LINE
Your fate line is flexible and changes direction, reflecting career changes within an organization rather than between companies. The clarity and depth of the line shows you are someone who changes direction when your career does not go as planned.

SUCCESS LINE
The success line springing from the Mars negative mount translates as success coming from your professionalism and integrity.

HEALTH NOTE
The cracked pattern of negative stress lines over your palm could, in part, be because of your type of head line pushing you onward.

⬛ HEAD LINE

◆ ENDS IN UPWARD FORK

You have strong business acumen and a feel for successful business practices. Your head line itself is wavy, patchy in places, and has an island, which usually indicates a time of weakness. Your mind is easily distracted. The lightly etched appearance of the line suggests that thinking deeply or studying is a strain. This seems to be caused, in your case, by ill health, shown by the island and other similarly affected lines.

MERCURY LINE
The line running from your Venus mount diagonally across your palm to your little finger is the Mercury or health line, indicating that you should take care of your health.

COMPLEMENTARY READINGS

LIFE LINE
Four episodes of trauma are evident in the health-related trauma lines that show as patches on your life line. The last period of trauma seems to be in your early thirties, when your life hits a long, clear spell.

HEAD LINE ⬛

VIA LASCIVIA
The via lascivia, or allergies line, is a deep line across your palm from the edge opposite the thumb. In such a potentially sensitive palm, this may mean you develop allergies to previously tolerated drugs.

◆ ENDS IN DOWNWARD FORK

Known as a writer's fork when below the ring finger, this downward fork denotes a commercially successful creative talent. The branch is fairly level and does not dip too sharply, which suggests nonfiction creative writing. Your head line starts independently of the life line but is tied to it with a latticework of branching lines. This shows that you are alternately confident and hesitant, a trait that can be overcome if your life and head lines run parallel for no more than an inch.

COMPLEMENTARY READINGS

DROPLETS
Droplets on all fingertips show exceptional sensitivity. A rare sign of extraordinary talent, legend has it that with this gift you can "feel" colors.

FATE LINE
Starting from the Venus mount inside the life line, your fate line tells of early family commitments. You are possibly a parent wanting success through or for your children. A radical change in your thirties brings a new career direction.

STAR
The star on your Apollo mount shows that you will achieve fame and fortune.

TEACHER'S SQUARE
The teacher's square on your Jupiter mount reveals a talent for instruction on almost any subject.

JUPITER MOUNT
A strong index finger and developed Jupiter mount show that ambition is strongly highlighted for you.

HEAD LINE

4.11 HEAD LINE

◆ TRIDENT END

You have extraordinary mental abilities. Business acumen, determination, and inspiration are your recipe for success. The branch to the Mars negative mount, on the outer edge of your palm, shows determination and fortitude; the branch to Luna mount shows inspiration and creativity; and the small branch deep into the Luna mount shows a complex imagination.

COMPLEMENTARY
READINGS

STAR
A star on your Apollo mount is a reliable sign of fame and fortune.

SOLOMON RING
A small Solomon ring on the base of your index finger denotes a natural aptitude for leadership and responsibility. Often people with this marking are pushed by others to lead because they do not seek leadership positions themselves.

HEAD LINE

FATE LINES
Double fate lines could mean you have two careers running side by side, or that you undertake prospect-enhancing study part-time while working.

BRANCH
The branch from your life line to your Saturn mount is an unusual feature and shows a massive, ultimately successful effort to achieve something of major importance to you.

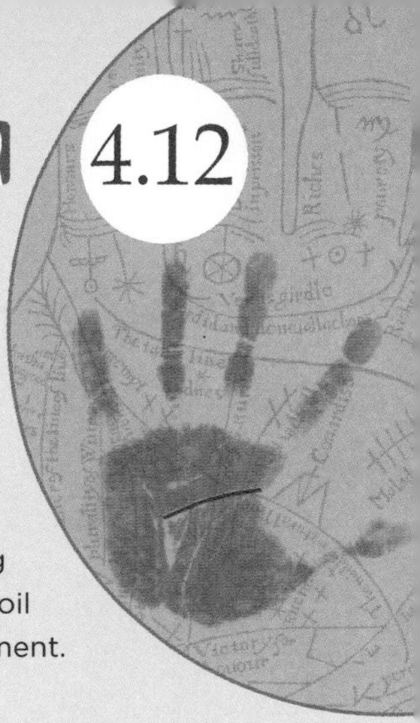

◆ DOUBLE
◆ PART OR FULL

A sure sign of brainpower, the double head line is seen here as part of a pseudo-simian line. A double head line is normally interpreted by combining the qualities of each individual line. Your upper line curves down toward the Luna mount, showing a creative predisposition. Your lower line is straight, directed toward the outer edge of the palm, showing a logical intellect. You are capable both of great turmoil and massive achievement.

COMPLEMENTARY READINGS

BLUE NAIL POLISH
Blue nail polish could mean that you have an attraction to the mystical realm.

HEAD LINE

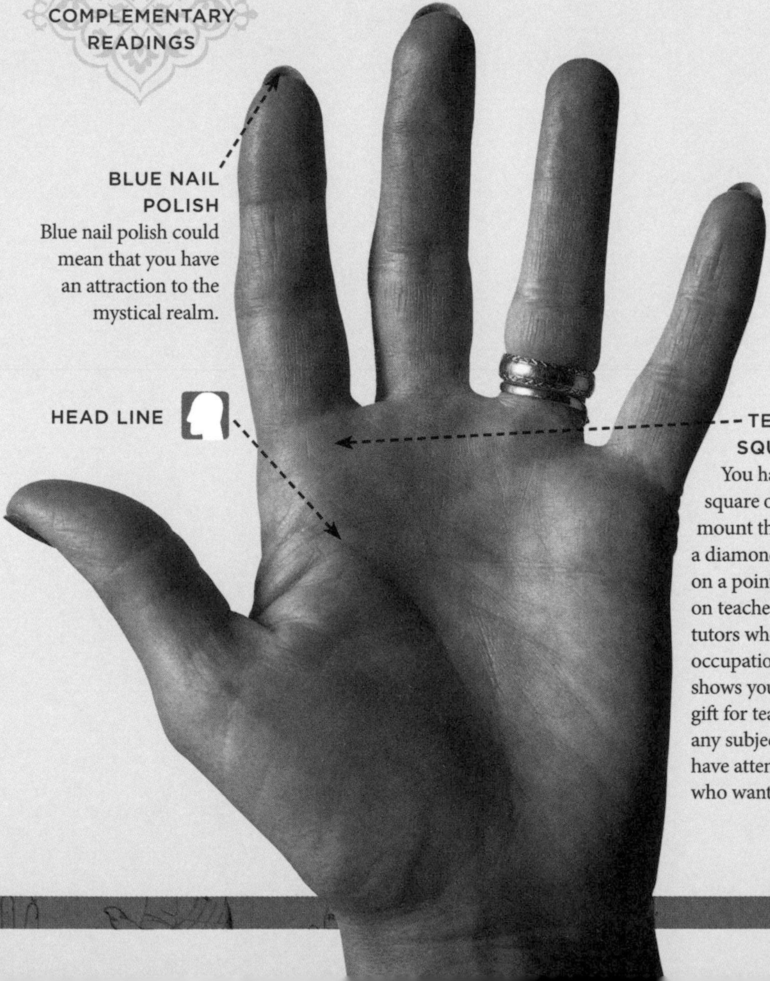

TEACHER'S SQUARE
You have a teacher's square on your Jupiter mount that looks like a diamond, as it stands on a point. Also present on teachers and tutors who love their occupation, this sign shows you have a real gift for teaching almost any subject, when you have attentive pupils who want to learn.

HEAD LINE

4.13 ⬛ HEAD LINE

♦ **LONG**

♦ **DIPS SHARPLY**

You have a great imagination, which if suppressed, could lead to depression. With the head line deep in your Luna mount, you are prone to hypersensitivity and must use your creative energies or they are likely to consume you. Your clear, long head line shows clarity of vision. Bridging lines at the start of your life line express confidence with periods of self-doubt. A common-sense appreciation of talent will cause this latticework to fade over time.

COMPLEMENTARY READINGS

PALMAR RIDGES
A tri-radii palmar ridge pattern on the Mercury and Jupiter mounts gives intensity to these areas. Communication and leading innovation are strongly highlighted for you.

ATTACHMENT LINE
Your attachment line has a fork with an exceptionally long, continuing branch, suggesting a soul mate.

HEAD LINE ⬛

HEART LINE
Your heart line ends strongly on the index finger, showing that you idealize partners. A lesser branch falling back to the life line reflects the intensity you give your life's work.

TOP PHALANX
The tapered top phalanx of your thumb shows sensitivity to moods, people, and emotions.

HEAD LINE

◆ DOMINANT
◆ DIFFERENT FROM PASSIVE

There are fundamental differences between these right and left hands. While the left palm shows a long head line dipping into the Luna mount, the right hand head line has branches to the Mars negative mount. On the passive hand, this means inner determination. A branch from the life line through the start of the head line shows that you are destined for success, with the loop of inspiration on your Luna mount revealing an excess of talent.

COMPLEMENTARY READINGS

LIFE LINE
A double life line on this passive hand, faint but present, means that you have the potential for a very different life. This alternative life has not been followed as it does not appear in the dominant left hand, which represents current, actual life.

ATTACHMENT LINES
Attachment lines show up as two long lines, revealing the possibility of soul mate partners. The second partner will not materialize, as there is just one partner shown in the dominant hand.

HEAD LINE

SIMIAN LINE

What does this unique
hand marking mean?

LOCATION

The simian line runs from between the index finger and the thumb, straight across the hand to finish on the outer edge under the little finger. It appears as a horizontal line, which is actually the head line and the heart line fused together, making the direction of how to read it very difficult.

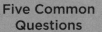

MEANING

The simian line appears to cut straight across the palm, from between the thumb and index finger across to the outer edge, and is actually a head and heart line fused together. A simian line is often, though not exclusively, associated with Down's syndrome. When seen in a non-Down's syndrome hand, it signifies extraordinary intensity and powers of achievement. A simian line indicates a focused and forceful person who is an excellent achiever, but someone who has difficulty relating emotionally. Einstein was rumored to have a simian line. Possessiveness and jealousy in relationships can be a problem for such individuals. The presence of a head and/or heart line softens some of the characteristics of the simian line and it is then known as a pseudo-simian line.

Five Common Questions

◆ Why do I have to do everything perfectly?

◆ Why do I feel different from others?

◆ If I don't have a heart line, does it mean I am unfeeling or will be unlucky in love?

◆ Will I achieve what I set out to do?

◆ Will I always live my life with such intensity?

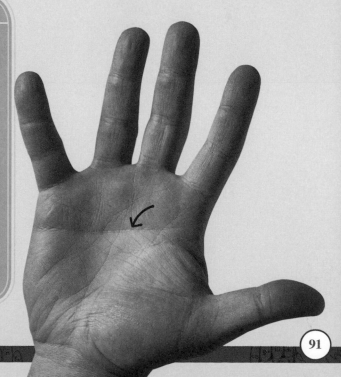

♥ SIMIAN LINE

♦ **STRAIGHT ACROSS PALM**
♦ **NO HEART OR HEAD LINE**

You are an individual whose concentrated mental energies are applied with laserlike intensity—you simply cannot be disturbed when absorbed in a task. You are essentially a major achiever. A heavily chained simian line tells of difficulties in your life. The fate line extending to your index finger points to success in business, with the long top phalanx of your thumb indicating great willpower and determination.

**SYMPATHY/
EMPATHY LINES**
Many sympathy/empathy lines show you care deeply.

**COMPLEMENTARY
READINGS**

LIFE LINE
Your apparently short life line with a line connecting to the fate line points to an emigration early in life after some trauma. The clarity of the continuing line means your life gets easier.

**GIRDLE
OF VENUS**
A full girdle of Venus shows the sensitivity, compassion, and sensuality in your nature. A coiled spring, you have an abundance of nervous energy, as illustrated by the branched appearance.

STRESS LINES
Negative stress lines cover your hand, including exhaustion lines up the fingers. These can be controlled, though with your determination to see a project through, they are likely to return again and again.

♥ **SIMIAN
LINE**

♦ **WITH HEART LINE**
♦ **WITH HEAD LINE**

Intensity and concentrated mental energies that are never applied halfheartedly are your trademarks. You dislike being disturbed when absorbed in a task, which usually results in successful completion of the task. You prefer one task at a time. A major achiever, your heart and head lines soften a potentially hard approach to other people and ideas.

COMPLEMENTARY READINGS

ISLANDS
This pattern on all your fingers is a major sign that you are someone who will be or is extremely successful. Combined with the simian nature of your hand, these fingertips reveal a truly indomitable character.

HEAD LINE
Starting linked to your life line by a pattern of latticework, your head line shows spurts of confidence followed by periods of self-doubt. Self-assurance will go a long way toward negating these feelings. If the negative feelings are overcome, these lines will fade in time.

MERCURY LINE
This line, starting from your Venus mount and sweeping toward your little finger, is usually a health warning of some kind. It cuts across an early fate line, allowing a second fate line from the Luna mount to take over.

♥ **SIMIAN LINE**

♥ SIMIAN LINE

- ◆ **STRAIGHT ACROSS PALM**
- ◆ **NO HEART OR HEAD LINE**
- ◆ **PASSIVE**
- ◆ **SAME ON BOTH HANDS**

You apply concentrated mental energies with laserlike intensity. Never halfhearted, you simply cannot be disturbed when absorbed in a task. You are likely to be extremely gifted intellectually. With simian lines on both hands, the effects are multiplied, making you extremely successful.

MYSTIC CROSS
The mystic cross highlights a highly developed intuition that can mean a talent for speculative business deals.

COMPLEMENTARY READINGS

AMBITION LINE
The line coming from the life line toward the Jupiter mount shows successful completion of a heartfelt ambition.

♥ **SIMIAN LINE**

LIFE LINE
Your life line has a slightly difficult start, but this passive hand shows fewer obstacles than in your dominant hand, revealing a more awkward but ultimately exciting path in life.

MERCURY LINE
This branch line, from your life line to your little finger, shows a health issue that needs attention. On your dominant hand, however, this line appears as a business line coming from the fate line.

FATE LINE
Rising branches on this line mean that you will become self-employed.

SIMIAN LINE ♥

- ◆ **STRAIGHT ACROSS PALM**
- ◆ **NO HEART OR HEAD LINE**
- ◆ **DOMINANT**

You are highly focused. Sometimes indicating Down's syndrome, this is also the mark of a major achiever. You are likely to be gifted intellectually. The simian line is thought to be formed by a fusion of the head and heart lines, giving you the potential to be totally self-centered and subjective in your dealings. You have a strong need for secure material foundations.

COMPLEMENTARY READINGS

SIMIAN LINE ♥

AMBITION LINE
This line that moves from the life line toward the Jupiter mount shows success in a lifelong ambition.

LIFE LINE
Your life line has a difficult start with a number of crossing lines in childhood. Trauma lines scattered throughout your life keep you on your toes but do not bowl you over. A fork in your line around the age of forty shows an emigration or major change following a tough decision.

FATE LINE
A significant opportunity in your forties causes a change in career direction, shown by the change in line direction. The doubled line and the stars on the main line light the way for change and help you to shine.

MERCURY LINE
A branch line from the fate line to the little finger shows that success in your career depends on insight and inspiration.

FATE LINE

Are you in the
right career?

LOCATION

The fate line starts on the center part of the palm just above the wrist and usually travels up the palm toward the middle finger. Read the fate line in this direction.

MEANING

The fate line gives information about your career, how you feel about it, and whether it is challenging you. A straight, clear, deep line indicates a long and successful career. A line that stops and starts, running clearly, then faintly, shows career twists and turns. A line cutting clearly across the fate line may indicate that you are being searched out for a specific job. This section describes and illustrates many palms with variations to the fate line.

Five Common Questions

- Did I choose the right career?
  - Will I be head-hunted?
- Will I achieve my ambition of working for myself?
  - My working life seems to be constantly changing; will it settle down in the future?
    - Should I take up an new, exciting career that is being offered to me?

FATE LINE

- ◆ **STRAIGHT**
- ◆ **CLEARLY DEFINED**

You have a strong, vocational, job-for-life line. A possible new career opportunity, shown as a rising branch, appears in your twenties. The new job is not pursued as the line does not change direction, but your continuing career appears much stronger and more fulfilling. Your index finger is very thick, showing natural leadership and business sense, with your little finger held apart denoting independence of thought.

STAR
A star on the Apollo mount stands for fame and fortune. Combined with your other features, you have the ingredients of an excellent politician.

COMPLEMENTARY READINGS

HEAD LINE
Your head line dipping sharply into your Luna mount shows that you must use your strong, creative powers of imagination.

FATE LINE

INTUITION LINE
Your intuition line starts with a star on the Luna mount, highlighting inspired business decisions.

LOOPS OF VOCATION AND HUMOR
Loops of vocation and humor show you are a hardworking, fun person to have around.

◆ **APPEARS TO STOP AND START**

You will have numerous changes of career or employer, due in many cases to boredom, frustration, or lack of challenges. The girdle of Venus adds nervous energy to your need to change direction. A heart line branch thrown downward to the head line acts like a simian line, pushing you with intensity to focus on new challenges. This may have the result of turning you into a workaholic or a nervous wreck.

COMPLEMENTARY READINGS

ISLANDS
The island fingerprint pattern on a number of fingers is another strong sign of success. You have the ability to make an island of yourself and focus successfully on projects. Success is most likely through working on your own, not as part of a team.

FATE LINE

CHILDREN LINES
Your children lines are numerous and deep, like those seen on pediatricians and teachers. With this level of empathy, working with children is recommended.

SUCCESS LINE
Your success line shows some early successes where it mirrors the fate line, but most recognition will come later in life.

FATE LINE

6.3 FATE LINE

◆ STARTS HIGH ON PALM

You will only start a career, or begin to feel secure in your chosen career, later in life. There are actually two fate lines visible, with the shorter one starting in your thirties and ending around the age of fifty. This line, rather than representing a second career, thwarts aims and ambitions along its length. The main career line, to the left of the shortened line, suffers some faintness and changing of direction while the shorter line is active. Later in life, when you enjoy some success, the success line mirrors the main fate line.

COMPLEMENTARY READINGS

TRAUMA LINES
Many trauma lines cross the life line until the mid-thirties, when your life seems to become more comfortable.

FATE LINE

LIFE LINE
Your double life line is fairly developed and similar in appearance to a line often seen on actors. In thespian terms, the double life represents home life and life on stage or screen.

VIA LASCIVIA
The via lascivia is fairly prominent on the lower part of your Luna mount. The hand itself is fairly delicate in appearance, with a stress patterning of fine lines. Any substances causing allergy or sensitivity should probably be avoided.

FATE LINE

◆ STARTS ON LUNA MOUNT

A career in the limelight or in politics would be the most suitable one for you. Palmists often have difficulty when interpreting hands full of stress lines, like this one, in picking out the main lines as clearly as possible. Your fate line is very deep and clear, running straight from the Luna mount to the index finger. In your potential career in the limelight, this indicates elements of pride and ambition, as well as a natural desire to promote yourself.

COMPLEMENTARY READINGS

INFLUENCE LINES
Two significant influence lines, one in your twenties and another in your fifties, run across your life line to the Mercury mount, showing you as strong and positive, open to opportunities for self-promotion in the media.

ULNAR LOOPS
Ulnar loops on all the fingers show your versatility and adaptability in wide-ranging situations.

SOLOMON RING
The Solomon ring around the base of your index finger shows a natural talent for leadership.

HEART LINE
Your short, straight, level heart line indicates that your partners know exactly where they stand in your life.

FATE LINE

FATE LINE

◆ STOPS FAR SHORT OF BASE OF FINGERS

Your fate line stops short at the heart line, indicating
that you may experience a sudden fortunate change in
circumstances, perhaps a lottery win or a chance windfall.
Other characteristics in your palm reinforce this—there seem
to be a lot of pointers to a possible lucky change of lifestyle.

STAR
A star on your Apollo
mount is a strong
indication of fame
and fortune.

**COMPLEMENTARY
READINGS**

HEAD LINE
Your head line ends in a
long fork, with a branch
to the Mars negative mount
highlighting determination
and perseverance and a
branch to the Luna mount
showing creativity.

LIFE LINE
The early portion
of your life line shows
some disturbances, but
it becomes much clearer
from the thirties onward.
A fork shows a major
change in circumstance or
an emigration around the
end of the fate line, with
a branch to the little finger
at the same point showing
a clearer business focus.

FATE LINE

FATE LINE

◆ **ENDS HIGH ON PALM**
◆ **STOPS AT BASE OF FINGERS**

You will either work, probably voluntarily, past retirement age or become engrossed in a retirement occupation. A fate line starting early and continuing all the way to the base of the fingers is always a sign of driving life energy. Your clear, strong fate line suggests that your job is fulfilling and challenging in its own right, and that you enjoy a high degree of success.

COMPLEMENTARY READINGS

FATE LINE

JUPITER MOUNT
A very developed Jupiter mount shows that you are highly ambitious.

MARS POSITIVE MOUNT
Mars positive has the appearance of a shallow lake, denoting your ability to assess people quickly and accurately.

VENUS MOUNT
Your well-developed Venus mount reinforces how important it is for you to maintain working contacts with people.

HEAD LINE
Your head line ends in a writer's fork below the ring finger, a sign that you will derive a lot of pleasure from the occupation of writing.

FATE LINE

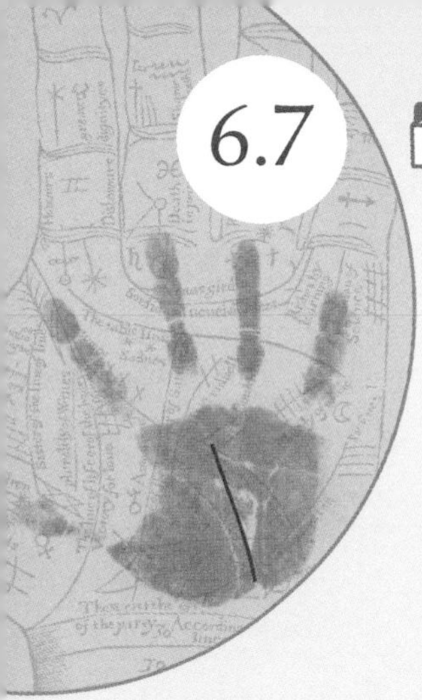

FATE LINE

◆ ENDS TOWARD INDEX FINGER

With natural ambition, pride, and self-promotion, you are likely to achieve great success. Your double fate line paints a picture of you working at your success, with the main career line going straight to and ending right on the Jupiter mount. Your success is guaranteed and will be earned through your own efforts.

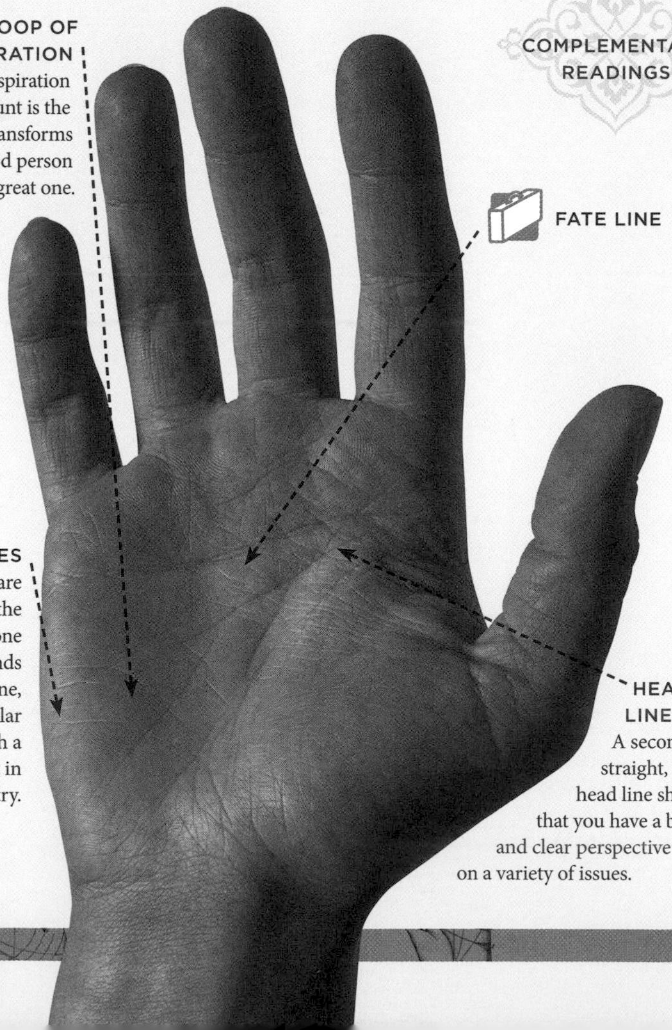

LOOP OF INSPIRATION
The loop of inspiration on the Luna mount is the element that transforms you from a good person into a great one.

COMPLEMENTARY READINGS

FATE LINE

TRAVEL LINES
Many travel lines are present next to the Luna mount, one of which extends to the fate line, representing regular dealings with a business contact in another country.

HEAD LINE
A second straight, clear head line shows that you have a balanced and clear perspective on a variety of issues.

♦ **WITH A LINE STRIKING IT**
♦ **UPWARD JOINING BRANCH**

The upward branch is a good indication of a positive career move. Two opportunities appear in your thirties, with the earlier one crossing the fate line without being pursued. This first branch, going toward the Mercury mount, is the business line, showing that you have a strong edge in commercial dealings. The stock market is full of people with business lines. The career opportunity branch changes the direction of the fate line slightly.

COMPLEMENTARY READINGS

ISLANDS
Island fingerprint patterns on your ring and little fingers show great achievements in the world of money, fun, and communications.

LOOPS OF VOCATION AND HUMOR
Loops of vocation and humor show that you have a lovely, rounded personality.

RAJA LOOP
A raja loop present between the index and middle fingers is both rare and significant. You may have a direct blood connection to royalty, and are likely to have a regal attitude and refined tastes.

FATE LINE

SUCCESS LINE
Your success line does not, oddly enough, mirror the fate line, showing that success and recognition in your life appear to come from entirely different angles.

LIFE LINE
A branch from the life line shooting to the Jupiter mount points to ambition and success.

FATE LINE

FATE LINE

◆ STARTS ON VENUS MOUNT

Your career is probably tied in some way to your family. In addition to the one on the Venus mount, your fate line has a number of other starts, which combine into one line and career around your late twenties or early thirties. Multiple starter branches usually signify courses of study combined with career. This palm is not so simple. With your multiple lines, you are likely to have many strings to your bow and be capable of pursuing many jobs successfully.

COMPLEMENTARY
READINGS

BRANCH
A branch from the center of your palm straight to the Jupiter mount shows leadership talents and business success.

LIFE LINE
A partially double life line points to a second, exciting, and successful career that you will take up in the future.

SUCCESS LINE
Your success line, sweeping from the Luna mount and running parallel to the main fate line, shows a successful career with a good degree of public exposure and recognition.

FATE LINE

FATE LINE

◆ MULTIPLE ENDS

Multiple fate lines reflect the running of several careers at the same time. Just after crossing your head line, sometime in your fifties, your fate line breaks into a number of lines. You will probably enter a period of self-employment or run a business, undertaking multiple roles yourself. The strength of the lines suggests business success. The continuation of the central line or role, and the success lines, reinforce this pattern.

COMPLEMENTARY READINGS

AMBITION LINES
Running upward from the start of the life line, these represent lifelong academic ambitions that have been or will be achieved.

JUPITER MOUNT
Your well-developed Jupiter mount shows that you focus on ambition, pride, leadership, and honor. You believe in your own worth, but as the mount is not overdeveloped, you are also fully aware of your faults.

FATE LINE

INTUITION LINE
Running almost parallel to the business line near the outer edge of your palm, your intuition line shows you have an extra dimension of imagination and people awareness.

BUSINESS LINE
Peeling from the lower part of the life line and running toward the little finger is a business line, or Mercury line. The growth and success of your career or business depends on a business sixth sense to keep you one step ahead of the market.

FATE LINE

◆ DOUBLED FOR ANY OF ITS LENGTH

This can indicate running more than one career or job simultaneously, but it can also indicate an intensive course of study being undertaken while in a job. You probably have two careers running side by side, or two distinct parts to one job. In your fifties, the creative, imaginative job becomes more prominent and possibly more fulfilling, but this ceases around the age of sixty. Your original career, which involves people, will bring you the most success; that part of the fate line is mirrored by the success line.

DOUBLE WHORL
A double whorl fingerprint pattern on the index finger indicates a strong sense of balance. You weigh issues and chances when making decisions.

COMPLEMENTARY READINGS

SOLOMON RING
The Solomon ring on a strong index finger suggests you will take over either the whole of a business, or part of it.

 FATE LINE

BUSINESS LINE
The business line, springing from the life line and running toward the Mercury mount, shows you have a strong feel for business success. This line tends to appear around the time your career takes off.

TOP PHALANX
The top phalanx of your thumb is bulbous, showing a possible obsessive side to your personality, but the lower phalanx is fairly long and logical, balancing any obsessive excesses with good reasoning powers.

FATE LINE

◆ DOUBLED FOR ANY OF ITS LENGTH

This can indicate running more than one career simultaneously, or an intensive course of study being undertaken while in a job. Your main fate line starts almost at the wrist, in the Neptune area, showing your desire to work with people. The second fate line, to the left, starts on the Luna mount and demonstrates your persistent desire for public recognition. Your fate lines are angled differently until you are into your forties, but the different experiences you have will provide new ideas.

COMPLEMENTARY READINGS

HEAD LINE
A double head line shows you have the double blessing of intellectual capacity and a gift for seeing both sides of a problem. The higher line is straightforward, enabling you to tackle theoretical ideas easily. The lower line is wavy, denoting sporadic concentration, with the overlapping break showing a loss of continuity in following up ideas.

LUNA MOUNT
Your lower Luna mount is well-developed, almost hanging over the wrist, which reveals your interest in the paranormal. This is often the sign of a psychic.

FATE LINE

FATE LINE

FATE LINE

◆ **STARTS FROM LIFE LINE**
◆ **PASSIVE**

Starting from a point on the life line and running toward the middle finger, your fate line shows a family-related career. The line splits into multiple lines in your fifties, representing self-employment. Being right-handed, these life indications on your left, passive hand are equivalent to an itinerary for a journey. Your actions on the actual journey may change. If the same features appear on your dominant right hand, you have followed or will follow your predicted plan.

TEACHER'S SQUARE

A teacher's square on your Jupiter mount looks like a diamond, as it stands on a point. Also found on teachers and tutors who love their occupation, this sign shows you have a real gift for teaching almost any subject, when you have attentive pupils who want to learn.

COMPLEMENTARY READINGS

INDEX FINGERTIP

An island pattern on the tip of your index finger shows your ability to be single-minded in business. You are likely to be successful.

FATE LINE

SUCCESS LINE

Starting from the edge of the palm away from the thumb, and turning toward your ring finger, your success line shows kudos and prestige coming from your work for or with the public.

HEALTH NOTE

The top rascette, or bracelet, of the wrist shows susceptibility to genital/urinary tract problems or infections.

FATE LINE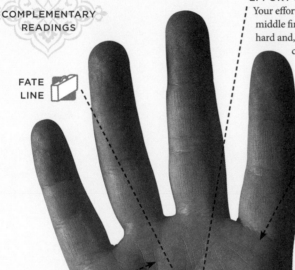

◆ **DOMINANT**
◆ **DIFFERENT FROM PASSIVE**

There are fundamental differences between your right, dominant palm and left, passive palm with its fate line originating from the life line and ending in multiple lines. Here, the fate line is fainter, with a second line from your Luna mount trying to join the main line. You seem to be resisting a family business or profession, and feel a lack of support. Any character indications mirrored in the passive hand will be strongly featured.

COMPLEMENTARY READINGS

FATE LINE

EFFORT LINE
Your effort line, from life line to middle finger, shows you work hard and, although nothing comes easily, your efforts are rewarded.

SOLOMON RING
A Solomon ring is often a strong sign of leadership, but not always in a business field.

SUCCESS LINE
Fainter than on your left hand, your success line follows the same path. Kudos and prestige may come from your work for or with the public.

ANGLE OF TIMING
This pronounced angle reveals an impeccable sense of timing.

FATE LINE

SUCCESS LINE

Will fame and fortune
find you?

LOCATION

The success line is located between the fate line and the edge of the palm away from the thumb, and runs up the palm in the same direction as the fate line. Start from the middle of the palm just above the wrist and read the success line as it runs up the palm toward the ring finger. In the right hand, the success line will be to the left of the fate line. In the left hand, it usually runs to the right of the fate line.

MEANING

The success or sun line represents the successes in your life. It is usually short, but becomes significant when it seems to copy the fate line at the point of a career change, almost guaranteeing the success of that change. This section describes and illustrates many palms with variations to the success line.

Five Common Questions

- Will my new business succeed?
- Will I finally get the recognition I deserve?
- Will I win the sweepstakes or lottery?
- I have had a number of promotions and raises. Is this going to "run out"?
- Will I always have to work hard for my success?

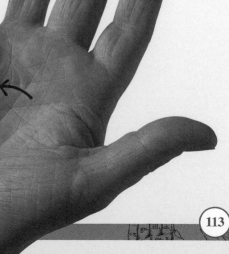

SUCCESS LINE

- ◆ **SHORT**
- ◆ **STARTS IN TOP HALF OF PALM**

You will achieve a long-desired ambition later in life. Although your success line only starts in earnest in your fifties, its clarity suggests great success in terms of promotion, prestige, or remuneration.

MARS LINE
Your Mars line, running inside the life line close to the thumb, acts as a guardian angel. Concurrent with a period of career changing, the line appears just when you need it. Your problems do not disappear, but you bounce back and make the best of your situation.

COMPLEMENTARY READINGS

HEAD LINE
The start of your head line is independent of your life line, showing independence from an early age and a tendency to be adventurous and impulsive. The high start indicates your ambitious nature. You are highly motivated and capable of great achievement.

FATE LINE
Overlapping starts to your fate line show you feeling your way for the right career path. The line splits into many lines later in life, showing self-employment coinciding with the time of your greatest success.

SUCCESS LINE

SUCCESS LINE 📚

◆ FAINT

Either you are not sufficiently appreciated or you perceive a lack of recognition. Your success line appears patchy, with some success in your twenties and thirties, but the clearest line, and the bulk of your success, will come later in life. You have many developed mounts, suggesting that you reach out to life in almost every way.

APOLLO MOUNT
You have a sunny disposition, with a sense of humor and a prevailing sense of resilient optimism.

COMPLEMENTARY READINGS

RINGS
A ring on your middle finger shows a yearning for security; on your ring finger, a strong commitment to partnerships; and on your little finger, a covert need to control.

JUPITER MOUNT
You believe in yourself and have a strong sense of ambition and justice.

SUCCESS LINE 📚

LUNA MOUNT
The Luna mount overhangs the wrist, showing you are creative, artistic, and mysterious.

FATE LINE
A problem in your fifties, possibly affecting your health, shows as a star where your fate line crosses your head line. The resolution of the problem is unusual, evidenced by the starburst pattern on the fate line.

SUCCESS LINE

SUCCESS LINE

◆ STARTS WITH A STAR

You are virtually guaranteed success. This mark is often seen on the hands of fortune winners. Your success line starts with a star on the Luna mount, and another star appears at the start of the second part of the line.

ARCH
All your fingertips show an arch pattern, signifying a strong desire to make everyone and everything protected and secure.

COMPLEMENTARY READINGS

LIFE LINE
A break and reconnection of the life line in your mid to late forties shows a potential emigration or a radical change in circumstances. From this point, your fate line represents your life line. As it sweeps wider around the thumb, so your prospects open out.

SUCCESS LINE

NEPTUNE MOUNT
A well-developed Neptune mount shows you are in tune with the world, able to understand and empathize with the feelings of others. Quick, perceptive, and charismatic, your type of magnetic personality is often found in entertainers and public speakers.

SYMPATHY/ EMPATHY LINES
You have a great deal of empathy with the suffering of others, which is shown by the parallel lines running across your Jupiter mount.

◆ AS THREE LINES
◆ UPWARD FROM HEART LINE

You will have a guaranteed income, but will have to work for it. A success line in this position really has an effect later in life, with a certain amount of gratifying recognition. Your long fate line shows that, although the ability to earn will always be there, success will usually be because of your own efforts. The length of your fate line shows you have a driving need to be gainfully employed.

COMPLEMENTARY READINGS

GIRDLE OF VENUS
A partial girdle of Venus shows underlying nervous tension.

LITTLE FINGER
Your little finger leans away from your ring finger, showing a conflict of loyalties. Devotion to home or parents and the strong desire for independence usually results in guilt, with neither desire fully satisfied.

LUNA MOUNT
Your Luna mount appears developed but is unusually low set, showing a strong interest in or experience of the paranormal.

SUCCESS LINE

SUCCESS LINE

SUCCESS LINE

- ◆ **MULTIPLE**
- ◆ **REFLECTS FATE LINE**

You are assured success in the new business venture indicated in your fate line. Your fate line initially splits into two around the age of fifty, and shortly afterward, splits into many lines, signifying multitasking. You are more likely to run a company than to become self-employed. At such a potentially risky time, the best success line will reflect the fate line closely.

SUCCESS LINE

COMPLEMENTARY READINGS

AMBITION LINE
Running from the start of your life line is an ambition or achievement line. You will achieve a lifelong academic ambition.

THUMB
Your strong thumb, index finger, and little finger combine to show a powerful intellect.

LITTLE FINGER
Your firmly rooted, strong, thick little finger shows you communicate easily. The thick, lower phalanx shows you crying out for independence.

ANGLE OF TIMING
The pronounced angle where the lower phalanx of your thumb meets your palm shows you have an impeccable sense of timing. You are always in the right place at the right time. You are never late for an appointment.

♦ **MULTIPLE**
♦ **REFLECTS FATE LINE**

Your success line makes you assured of success in the new business venture indicated in your fate line. Your fate line initially splits into two around the age of fifty, and shortly afterward, splits into many lines, signifying multitasking.

COMPLEMENTARY READINGS

SUCCESS LINE 💵

TEACHER'S SQUARE
Your Jupiter mount has a low-set teacher's square. Many teachers who love their occupation also possess this sign. It reveals a person who has an aptitude for teaching.

AMBITION LINE
The line running from your life line to your index finger confirms that you will achieve lifelong academic ambitions.

FATE LINE
Your fate line starts deep in the Luna mount, suggesting a persistent desire for public recognition. A career that involves close contact with the public will help satisfy this desire for fame.

HEAD LINE
Your head line branches, with the main branch dipping sharply into your Luna mount. Known as a writer's fork, this indicates a commercially successful creative talent.

SUCCESS LINE

◆ **DOMINANT**
◆ **DIFFERENT FROM PASSIVE**

There are fundamental differences between this passive left hand and the dominant right hand with its long success line. The negative stress lines are also in evidence on your left palm, but your success and fate lines are different. The success line comes from inside the life line, which usually involves a catch or snag somewhere, and your fate line is very disjointed. The potential life map shown in your passive hand would have left you feeling very dissatisfied.

TEACHER'S SQUARE
The teacher's square on the Jupiter mount shows that you have the gift of imparting information.

COMPLEMENTARY READINGS

ISLANDS
The island fingerprint pattern appears on all the fingers of your passive hand, showing a need to achieve.

HEAD LINE
The long, straight head line, the Sydney line, is even more straight and focused on your passive hand, showing your inner determination.

SUCCESS LINE

HEART LINE
Doubling of the heart line reflects your dominant hand. This is very important, as discrepancies between the hands in attitudes to relationships usually mean that you attract people who are not suitable for you.

LUNA MOUNT
Your low, developed Luna mount is consistent in both palms, reinforcing your interest in the paranormal.

◆ LONG

Your work with or for the public brings you both prestige and recognition. Negative stress lines of long standing are in evidence across your palm, which is perhaps no surprise given the clear amount of work and success you have. Your success line is thick, rich, and clear, starting to mirror the fate line early and continuing to do so.

COMPLEMENTARY READINGS

ISLAND
An island fingerprint pattern on your index fingertip describes the focus and single-mindedness that ensure your success.

HEART LINE
The end of the second line of your double heart line shows you as a sensualist, with the complete line ending at the index finger making you a romantic.

TEACHER'S SQUARE
The teacher's square on the Jupiter mount shows your great aptitude for conveying information.

LUNA MOUNT
A low, developed Luna mount contradicts your otherwise material and grounded palm, by signifying an interest in the paranormal.

HEAD LINE
Your long, straight head line is a Sydney line, which translates as fierce intensity and focus. You go all out to succeed.

SUCCESS LINE

ATTACHMENT LINE

How many loves
will you have?

LOCATION

Attachment lines are located on the outer edge of the palm (away from the thumb), above and parallel to the heart line and below the ring that forms around the base of the little finger. The line closest to the heart line refers to your first attachment, with any further lines representing later relationships. The whole area is fairly small, so it is difficult to study accurately. The positions of the lines can be more significant than the lines themselves.

MEANING

Attachment lines, also known as marriage, relationship, and love lines, show the romantic attachments in your life, from your first true love to later marriages or relationships. It is very important to realize that not all the attachment lines mapped out in your dominant hand will necessarily correspond to significant attachments. If a relationship or marriage is successful, future attachment lines may fade over time. Comparing the lines on a person's dominant hand, which charts what is actually happening, with those on the passive hand, which shows the life map, can be immensely enlightening.

Five Common Questions

- Did I choose the right partner?

- Can I save my rocky marriage?

- In later life, will I be as happy and content with my partner as I am right now?

- Can I stop myself from being unfaithful despite the markings on my palm?

- I am unattached; will I find a new partner?

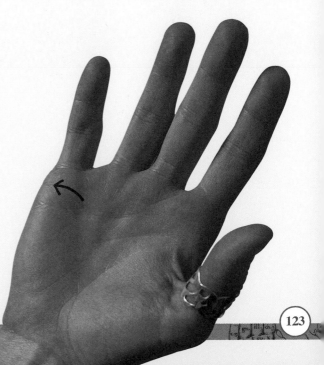

◆ FORKED END

Your long-standing relationship or marriage may dissolve, a move that may be initiated by you. It is always important to look for underlying causes and for areas that can be changed when problems are identified. In this example, the end is forked now, but the fork may fade if you make appropriate changes. On your passive hand, the fork is less likely to fade, as this palm shows the map of your potential in life and your opportunities. When you make major changes, or when opportunities open up, these are reflected in your dominant hand.

COMPLEMENTARY
READINGS

FATE LINE
Your fate line shows a period of unrest around the age of fifty, with your career branching out as a possible result. Could this put a strain on your marriage or partnership?

MARS LINE
The Mars line running inside your life line for a long way provides a safe environment in which to take chances, and certainly covers the age period around your fifties.

ATTACHMENT LINE ◑

TRAVEL LINES
Travel lines show in abundance on the edge of your palm away from the thumb. A number of the lines sweep toward your fate line, suggesting that much of the travel is business related.

ATTACHMENT LINE 🔗 8.2

◆ **HAS BREAK IN IT**
◆ **REJOINS**

Your relationship has a break and a subsequent reconciliation. Sometimes this marking indicates a couple living separate lives as opposed to separating physically. The break and overlap of the lines continue for some length, showing that perhaps the cement bonding your relationship needs to be reapplied frequently.

COMPLEMENTARY READINGS

HEART LINE
The rising and falling branches on your heart line show either a lot of early dating or that you want radically different things from your relationship from day to day. A relationship that survives these demands deserves to be valued. The fraying of the line shows a possible nervous disorder, which could be susceptibility to negative stress. The end of the line on your Jupiter mount shows you are vulnerable and inclined to the romantic side of life.

LIFE LINE
Your life line runs close to your thumb, revealing that you keep your feelings to yourself. Your head and life lines temper your sensitivity and can make you withdrawn and aloof.

GIRDLE OF VENUS
A partial girdle reflects your nervousness and anxiety but this is, after all, the flip side to your sensitivity to others and to your environment.

ATTACHMENT LINE 🔗

ATTACHMENT LINE

◆ **DIPS**
◆ **RUNS DOWN PALM**

You have a difficult relationship, and your partner may initiate a break. However, your attachment line has a shallow dip, which shows that there is a good chance of turning back the clock and making the partnership or marriage work again.

RING
The little finger ring is a sure sign that you need to have or feel in control of people and situations. Usually this refers to passive rather than obvious control.

COMPLEMENTARY READINGS

LIFE LINE
The close cut life line shows that you are probably uncomfortable with too much togetherness or intimacy.

ATTACHMENT LINE

HEART LINE
Your heart line is low and fairly straight, showing a tendency to stand back and not get too involved. The end tending toward the head line denotes a workaholic and your large Jupiter mount points to ambition.

STRESS LINES
The many stress lines on your palm could be either the cause or result of your difficult relationship.

◆ **DIPS**
◆ **RUNS DOWN PALM**

You have a difficult relationship, and your partner may initiate a break. A short, straight heart line with many branches shows you have varying emotional needs. You can be intimate without emotional commitment.

COMPLEMENTARY READINGS

HEALTH NOTE
Heightened color of the fingertips would make a blood pressure checkup a good idea.

GIRDLE OF VENUS
A partial girdle of Venus reflects your earthy sensuality and nervous energy.

FINGERS
The open space between your fingers reveals your open personality, yet the thumb is held close, keeping feelings, thoughts, and emotions in check. Could this be a learned response as a result of being hurt?

LIFE LINE
Your life line is very faint in the middle years but connects to the fate line for a time, indicating a radical change of circumstances.

VENUS MOUNT
The well-developed Venus mount shows you to be a lovely, "people" person, with a lot of vitality.

ATTACHMENT LINE ⚭

ATTACHMENT LINE

ATTACHMENT LINE

◆ RISES SHARPLY

Your partner will do well in business in his or her own right. Your attachment line itself is not a long line, showing that circumstances could cause some physical or emotional separation. Your fate line and success line show you have a strong feel for business, and that you are likely to provide the support necessary to help your partner's success.

HEART LINE

Your heart line stops short, showing that equality with your partner and physical loving are essential to you, although the slight curve on the end does show a romantic edge.

COMPLEMENTARY READINGS

GIRDLE OF VENUS

Your partial girdle of Venus shows an earthy sensuality. You make the most of time spent with your partner.

TOP PHALANX

You have awesome powers of persuasion, which is reflected in the long top phalanx of your little finger.

ATTACHMENT LINE

SIBLING LINES

Sibling lines between your index finger and thumb appear as two to three long lines. Sibling lines point to close relationships with siblings or friends during adulthood.

◆ **STRAIGHT**
◆ **CLEAR**

A balanced line that does not dip, break, or have an island shows you have a normal, balanced relationship. The line is neither too short, nor too long. A short line implies either a superficial relationship or one that does not involve doing everything together. A very long line means that you stay with someone, possibly even a soul mate, for many years, which could keep your life devoid of other achievements.

HEAD LINE
The start of the line is independent of the life line, showing independence from an early age. As a child, you were self-willed, but your palm as a whole has a feeling of restraint, curbing any childhood excesses. Latticework bridging the start of the head and life lines betrays periods of both confidence and self-doubt.

COMPLEMENTARY READINGS

FINGERS
The base of your fingers form a straight line, indicating confidence, and your square fingers reveal independence.

HEART LINE
The ending between your index and middle fingers shows you are an out-and-out sensualist.

THUMB RING
Thumb rings are often worn by individuals who are drawn to alternative lifestyles.

ATTACHMENT LINE

HEALTH NOTE
Fine negative stress lines on your palm could be caused by continuous overwork.

GIRDLE OF VENUS
Your partial girdle shows that you transmit an earthy sensuality.

GIRDLE OF VENUS

Are you sensuous?

LOCATION

The girdle of Venus runs from between the index and middle finger, girdles the two middle fingers, and ends between the ring finger and little finger. It is more often seen as two lines or a number of smaller lines than one continuous line.

MEANING

Throughout the history of palmistry, the girdle of Venus has been seen as a sensuous feature, defining a person in touch with their senses. On a less than robust palm, the girdle of Venus is likely to signify a nervous, sensitive person who is easily hurt. In extreme cases, this may translate as neuroticism with overtones of mild paranoia.

Five Common Questions

◆ Why do sensual pleasures mean so much to me?

◆ What makes me sensitive to moods, situations, even auras?

◆ I am high-strung with lots of nervous energy, yet my family background is sedate and placid. What could account for this?

◆ How can I tell if a potential suitor will match my sensuality?

◆ Could my stormy relationship be due to my sensuous nature?

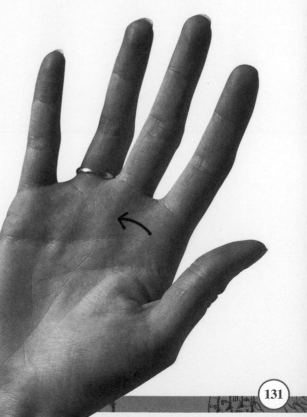

GIRDLE OF VENUS

- ◆ **FULL SEMICIRCLE**
- ◆ **AROUND BASE OF MIDDLE FINGERS**

You are extremely sensitive, compassionate, and sensual, and all your senses are highly attuned. You have a predisposition to display a lot of nervous energy and you are a go-getter. Having a double girdle of Venus doubles these characteristics, indicating you are very highly attuned to your senses, with a tendency toward oversensitivity. You are prone to allergies.

GIRDLE OF VENUS

COMPLEMENTARY READINGS

ATTACHMENT LINE
Your upper attachment line coincides with the fate line hot spot, showing a long, hectic, strong, and passionate relationship. Perhaps this attachment line refers to the partner responsible for the influence lines.

FATE LINE
Your fate line hits island and influence lines, showing career confusion and upheaval, but the line settles again, signaling the passing of the disturbance.

TOP PHALANX
The top phalanx of your thumb is tapered, pointing to sensitivity to atmosphere, moods, and people.

PALM
The long palm with long fingers shows you are an aesthetic, free-spirited individual with refined tastes.

GIRDLE OF VENUS

◆ CONNECTED TO ATTACHMENT LINE

You are likely to have a particularly stormy relationship. A full girdle of Venus sometimes results in feelings of insecurity and nagging doubts. A broken line, such as this one, shows you have some common sense. You do not jump immediately to negative conclusions, about the cancellation of a dinner date, for example. Although your potential for possessiveness and jealousy may sour a relationship, good, open communication will work wonders.

COMPLEMENTARY READINGS

HEART LINE
Your fairly short and straight heart line shows a susceptibility to fleeting affairs, although its low-set aspect reflects your guilty conscience, which is likely to stop most flirtations.

INTENSITY LINE
The line linking your head and heart lines is known as an intensity line. With reference to another person, it shows you may be head over heels in love. Regarding a career or special hobby, this intensity translates as heart and soul commitment.

GIRDLE OF VENUS

133

GIRDLE OF VENUS

◆ **PARTIAL**
◆ **SHORT BETWEEN INDEX/MIDDLE AND MIDDLE/RING FINGERS**

In addition to an earthy sensuality, a receptive attitude, and great sensitivity to others, you have a tendency to exhibit nervous energy. Your partner must either have similar markings or understand the reasons behind your attitudes and behavior.

RING
A ring on the middle finger shows your need for security and perhaps the emotional commitment of a stable marriage.

COMPLEMENTARY READINGS

GIRDLE OF VENUS

AMBITION LINE
You will achieve a heartfelt ambition.

HEART LINE
Long, curving, and romantic, your feminine heart line ends on your Jupiter mount, indicating romanticism and emotional vulnerability.

ATTACHMENT LINE
A dip toward the end of the line points to possible relationship difficulties resulting from your partner's stubbornness.

INFLUENCE LINE
An early, perhaps childhood, influence line crosses your life line and runs toward your index finger. An older and commanding person still seems to have influence over you.

GIRDLE OF VENUS

- ◆ **PARTIAL**
- ◆ **SHORT BETWEEN INDEX/MIDDLE AND MIDDLE/RING FINGERS**

In addition to an earthy sensuality, a receptive attitude, and great sensitivity to others, you have a tendency to exhibit nervous energy. Your partner must either have similar markings or understand the reasons behind your attitudes and behavior.

GIRDLE OF VENUS

LUNA MOUNT
The combination of developed Venus and Luna mounts reflects your trusting nature. You usually give others the benefit of the doubt.

ATTACHMENT LINE
Your relationship line breaks then rejoins, showing potential problems.

HEART LINE
Although short, your heart line has a gentle, romantic sweep. You need an equal partner who also possesses that touch of romanticism.

VENUS MOUNT
This well-developed Venus mount, showing sexuality and vitality, together with your partial girdle of Venus, shows you are physically loving and readily indulge in pleasure.

STRESS LINES

Do you suffer
from stress?

LOCATION

Stress lines tend to show up in all directions covering the palm. Lines radiating out from the base of the thumb will often be more obvious. Exhaustion lines running vertically up the fingers are also likely.

MEANING

Stress lines give a palm the appearance of cracked glaze on a vase. The palm appears full of fine lines, or of deeper lines with an overly smooth, dried out texture. Such a palm used to be known as a full palm or one that was full of life. This definition still holds true to some extent. However, today's stress lines are usually the result of negative stress. When the source of the negative stress is found and resolved, stress lines often start to fade rapidly, but they are likely to reoccur in people who push themselves too hard.

Five Common Questions

◆ How can I tell if negative stress is affecting me?

◆ How can I keep a check on my own level of stress?

◆ Are there parts of my personality that make me prone to stress?

◆ Can you tell the difference between recent stress and stress that has lasted years?

◆ If I exhibit stress now and deal with it, is it likely to recur in the future?

STRESS LINES

- ◆ **MANY STRONG LINES**
- ◆ **COVERING PALM**
- ◆ **PARTLY MASKING MAJOR LINES**

Strong covering lines denote negative stress that has accumulated over a period of time. The amount of stress that these lines express can seriously deplete your body's resistance to illness. To reverse the process, tackle the source of stress and the lines may fade over several months. If you are prone to stress, learn to recognize the signs in your hand and monitor them at regular intervals.

COMPLEMENTARY READINGS

PALM
Your palm shows a great deal of aggressive career drive and ambitious needs. Simply stepping back from your career could not only make you extremely unhappy but also potentially more stressed. Try meditation.

GIRDLE OF VENUS
Your girdle of Venus shows you are sensuous, but it also displays a certain amount of nervous tension and intensity, which should be kept in check.

STRESS LINES
Many strong lines cover the palm.

VIA LASCIVIA
The via lascivia running across your Luna mount is known as an allergies line. Your body is sensitive to many substances.

TOP PHALANX
The bulbous top phalanx of your thumb shows you are prone to obsessive behavior.

♦ **MANY FINE LINES**
♦ **COVERING PALM**
♦ **PARTLY MASKING MAJOR LINES**

Fine covering lines denote negative stress that is fairly recent
in onset. This hand shows the stress lines running up the
fingers and invading the fingertips comprehensively,
indicating that your glands could be affected and may not be
functioning fully. Adrenal overactivity can produce the
appearance of a full cover of lines.

COMPLEMENTARY
READINGS

SKIN
Your skin, particularly
at the fingertips, has an
appearance similar to a
hereditary condition
involving a missing
layer of skin.

HEART LINE
The branching
flick at the start
of the heart line
often appears at a
time of potassium
deficiency.

⚡ **STRESS LINES**
Many fine lines cover
the palm.

THUMB
Apparent
dryness of the flap
of skin connecting
your thumb to the
side of your hand
could point to
hormonal imbalances.

HEAD LINE
Your head line
dips very sharply,
which shows
your fantastic
creativity but also
low mood swings.

SPECIAL MARKINGS

SIGNS OF INTUITION

The bow of intuition and the mystic cross are strongly intuitive signs often found on the hands of psychics, mediums, and clairvoyants.

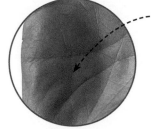

BOW OF INTUITION
This line is actually a Mercury or intuition line, which starts deep on the Luna mount, at the side of the palm away from the thumb, then runs up the hand and curves back toward the little finger.

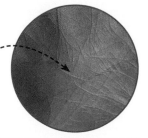

MYSTIC CROSS
The mystic cross is a distinct cross sign between the heart and head lines, often linking the two. Top people in large organizations have been found with this sign, denoting extra intuition and a gift for making the right decision.

LOOPS AND WHORLS

As the palmar ridges are fingerprint patterns on the hand, we also see the loops and whorls having a variety of meanings from their position.

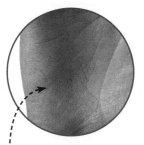

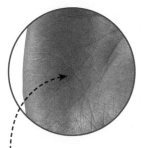

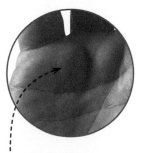

LOOP OF WATER
A loop going onto and toward the Luna mount, giving a strong affinity to water. Present in a notable round-the-world yachtsman.

LUNA WHORL
A circular stone dropped in a pond pattern found on the Luna mount shows a creative genius in the world of art and writing.

LOOP OF HUMOR
A loop between the ring and little finger is often possessed by comedians with a dry sense of humor.

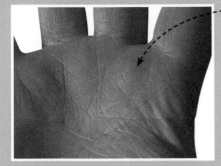

RAJA LOOP

The raja loop lies between the index and middle fingers and was historically a sign of noble blood in the family tree, with a direct link to royal blood. Even without conclusive evidence, a person with a raja loop is more likely to have refined tastes, and achieve a position of status and power.

SATURN RING

The Saturn ring is a second ring that runs around the base of the middle finger. Happily fairly uncommon, the Saturn ring shows up as a temporary line following a deep personal tragedy. A positive way to view this is that nature tries to keep a balance and will usually provide a strength to offset the negative feature.

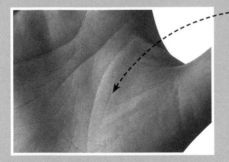

MARS LINE

This line is found running inside and next to the life line, for part of its length. Look for it away from the palm side, close to the thumb. The Mars line is like a guardian angel. It does not guarantee that you will not have problems in life, but it will push you back on your feet and moving again.

SOLOMON RING

This is a second ring that runs around the base of the index finger. Think of the Wisdom of Solomon to remember its meaning. A strong, thick index finger with a Solomon ring is also the sure sign of a leader, whether they naturally want to lead or they are pushed to the front to lead and organize.

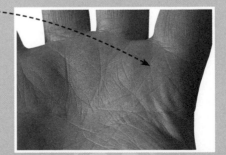

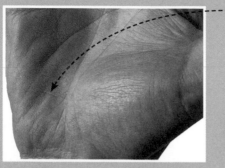

VIA LASCIVIA

Via lascivia looks like a heavier travel line running close to the wrist, usually appearing more like a crease. Historically, it was called a poison line and was thought to have dire properties attached to it. Today, it is more correctly considered as an allergies line, or a sign of hypersensitivity to certain foods, drinks, or drugs.

FRUSTRATION LINES

Frustration lines are distinct lines that run across the fingers. The source of frustration can be determined by the finger and the phalanx of the finger on which the lines are found.

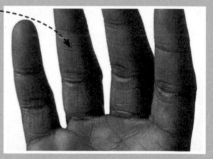

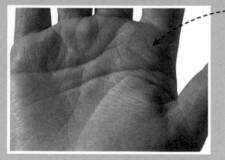

SYMPATHY LINES

Sympathy lines run straight across the base of the index finger. They are often found in members of the healing profession. More than one sympathy line can often mark a sympathy/empathy situation, where a person will suffer along with someone else and feel deeply on their behalf. Sympathy lines are always a sign of a very caring person even if there is a hard practical exterior.

TRAVEL LINES

Travel lines are lines found on the edge of the palm away from the thumb, close to the wrist, running back toward the thumb. They tell of a number of significant journeys but, interestingly, are not present where journeys are part of a job, such as for airline pilots. A travel line that touches the fate line stands for a foreign business connection.

INDEX

CREDITS

Quantum Books would like to acknowledge the following for supplying images reproduced in this book:

Mary Evans: p.11 (background palm) Illustrated London News

Shutterstock: p.10 bikeriderlondon

Wellcome Library, London: pp.7, 8, 17 (www.creativecommons. org/licenses/by/4.0)

Special thanks also to all the staff at Quarto, Quarto Children's Books, Quintet, Apple Press, and Artists & Illustrators for allowing us to photograph their hands for use in this book.

While every effort has been made to credit contributors, Quantum Books would like to apologize should there have been any omissions or errors and would be pleased to make the appropriate correction to future editions of the book.